ANTONIO
CARLUCCIO

antonio's
SIMPLE DISHES

PHOTOGRAPHY BY
ALASTAIR HENDY

ALHAMBRA
EDITIONS

PUBLISHING DIRECTOR Jane O'Shea
CREATIVE DIRECTOR Helen Lewis
PROJECT EDITOR Simon Davis
EDITOR Kathy Steer
EDITORIAL ASSISTANT Romilly Morgan
DESIGNER Katherine Keeble
PHOTOGRAPHER Alastair Hendy
PRODUCTION DIRECTOR Vincent Smith
PRODUCTION CONTROLLER
Sasha Taylor

First published as *Simple Cooking* in
2009 by Quadrille Publishing Limited
This edition first published in 2013 by
Alhambra Editions
Alhambra House
27-31 Charing Cross Road
London WC2H 0LS

Text © 2009, 2013 Antonio Carluccio
Photography © 2009 Alastair Hendy
Design and layout ©
  2013 Quadrille Publishing Ltd

Cataloguing in Publication Data: a catalogue
record for this book is available from the
British Library.

ISBN 978 184949 299 7

Printed in China

My culinary career began some 50 years ago while I was a student in Vienna. On a very low budget, and cooking for myself and friends, I had to learn very quickly how to stock a basic larder, how to buy fresh food wisely, cheaply, healthily and daily (as needed), and how to cook it simply. All my ideas came from a solid foundation: the years I had spent absorbing food facts, techniques, textures and tastes from my mother. She was a passionate family cook who managed to feed her large family well, creatively and very lovingly through the lean post-war years. Vegetables were cultivated in the garden, breads and pasta were made at home, and I was sent to forage for wild foods (I'm still wild about them, especially mushrooms). Nothing was wasted, and any leftovers were utilised in a dish for another day.

So, having been brought up in this wonderful way, I wasn't a complete novice in my Austrian kitchen. I had experienced at first hand how to put together dishes and meals with the minimum of ingredients for maximum flavour and satisfaction, and I knew that you didn't need a great deal of money to prepare good food for yourself. In Vienna, I spent a lot of time in the splendid *Naschmarkt*, a famous marketplace in the centre, where you could buy anything from fresh meat and fish, to freshly grown and picked vegetables and fruit from the countryside. There I could perfect the art of shopping and buying that I had begun to learn at home in Borgofranco.

It is interesting that once you are on your own, you develop a sense of self-sufficiency, and learn how to balance your working or studying time with good and valuable *free* time. In fact, at the same time as I was working happily, I learned to cook well, and discovered that producing food to share with friends (especially female friends) kept me socially busy and content. Those months in Vienna were very important for me, because they helped formulate the base of my future hobby/profession. Because of them, I am what I am today, a passionate, virtually self-taught cook with lots of experience in home cooking.

Although I have since been in charge of restaurants, front of house and in the kitchen, I have always preferred to 'observe', rather than 'run' (which I think enabled me to develop my skills more effectively). I have been lucky enough, through my career, to have visited thousands of Italian restaurants that have

let me put my nose in their kitchens to do just that. Often I have been invited to lunch with the Italian owners, and it has been fascinating for me to discover the variety of regional foods they have offered and to have engaged in discussions about the food of their area compared with others, either from the north or south.

All this has taught me to be impartial about Italian cuisine, giving preference to dishes that I particularly like, independent of the region they come from. Collecting so much information about Italian food has made me curious about its deeper cultural and historic origins, and I have written several books on the subject. The underlying theme behind all of them is the primary and most significant bit of knowledge that you will ever need to know about Italian food: that it is always very simple, and always uses the best ingredients possible.

So this book is a coming together of all the 'secrets' I have learned over those 50 years. Many of the recipes are traditional Italian, many are classics with a twist and some are my own inventions, but all are easy to achieve and delicious to eat. In some of them I reveal how you can make the recipe a little more special – by adding an extra flavour or ingredient – and in others I tell you how to utilise any leftovers to make another dish. Throughout, the recipes are punctuated with all sorts of culinary tips that I have picked up along the way.

This is a book for all those who would like to be able to cook real Italian food, and who perhaps are just starting on their own journey of culinary discovery. I firmly believe that cooking, whether for oneself, or for family and friends, is one of the most loving of human skills. I wish you good reading, successful cooking and great eating.

THE ITALIAN LARDER

If you are in Rome, Florence, Venice or Turin try to follow in the footsteps of a housewife out shopping. Italian housewives go to the local market every day, and you will be watching one of the world's greatest experts at food buying. You will learn that only the best ingredients produce the best food and, because she is so experienced, a look, and maybe a little touch, is all that's needed to gauge the quality.

Italian men do not usually get involved much in cooking, as they don't possess their wives' shopping acuity. I, however, helped out at an early age, as my mother thought we children – and there were six of us – should learn as soon as possible. One of the lessons I learned very quickly was that successful food shopping depends on the knowledge of the buyer. Once I was sent to the village butcher to buy some meat for a stew: I returned with sliced meat in a packet. My mother, furious, sent me back to the shop, and I needed all the charm of a 15-year-old about to be severely punished to convince the butcher to exchange the sliced meat for a piece…

The years I spent in Vienna as a bachelor, where I learned to cook properly, were the most influential, and the 'rules' I learned then have remained with me ever since. As well as the essentials and occasional luxurious extras (see below), I shopped every day for fresh fruit and vegetables, and with a few eggs or potatoes around, I never starved. Potatoes and canned or dried beans were very handy for making *pasta e patate or pasta e fagioli* (pasta and potatoes or pasta and beans). Meat was an occasional treat and the use of this and cheese was according to my budget (which at the time was very small indeed). I loved preparing soups and *minestrone* – and still do today – making use of leftovers from previous meals. Remember that food is far too precious to throw away.

The essential Italian larder of today need not be much more sophisticated than my original listing and it's still far better to shop for fresh foods as and when you need them. Always go for the best quality you can source. In your larder keep a little of everything you think you will need for making the dishes you like to cook and eat. To keep your larder functional from day to day, remember to replace what you have just used when you next go shopping, and periodically check that items haven't gone past their sell-by dates.

My essential Italian larder

Salt and black pepper
Sugar
Decent olive oil (ordinary for
    frying, extra virgin for raw)
Wine vinegar
Onions
Garlic
Some breadcrumbs
Pancetta (or ordinary bacon)
1 can beans in brine

Chilli (fresh or dried)
A few medium free-range eggs
Some potatoes
1 packet risotto rice
2 packets pasta (*linguine*
    and *penne*)
1 can peeled chopped tomatoes
Some chicken stock cubes (yes!)

'Luxurious' extras

Parmesan cheese
Dried porcini (ceps)
Speck (the equivalent of bacon,
    but air-dried and smoked)
Truffle oil
Balsamic vinegar
Anchovies in oil
Tuna in oil

starters
& SALADS

Sometimes, if you happen to sit in a Tuscan, Piedmontese or Roman *trattoria*, without asking for it you are served a bowl of crudités (called *cazzimperio* in Rome). These are whole or cut raw vegetables, usually the freshest of the season, often – a bit posh this – served on ice, along with a little bowl of virgin olive oil, salt, pepper and balsamic vinegar in which to dip. **PER PERSON (MULTIPLY AS NEEDED)**

raw vegetable crudités
WITH OIL & VINEGAR

To make the dip, place the oil, vinegar and garlic clove, if desired, into a bowl, adding a good pinch each of salt and pepper.

Arrange the vegetable pieces on a plate along with the dip. To serve, dip the vegetables into the oil and vinegar, being careful to stir the bottom and mix the ingredients together.

Serve with some good bread. So simple, but so delicious.

2 spring onions, carefully cleaned
2 tender celery stalks
2 thin slices fennel bulb
2 tender asparagus spears
1 young carrot, peeled and cut
   into batons
any other vegetables you might
   find interesting

Dip
about 2 tbsp olive oil
2 tbsp balsamic vinegar
1 garlic clove (optional),
   peeled and finely sliced
salt and pepper

This dish is a favourite of mine and can be eaten either as an *antipasto* or as an accompaniment for various dishes. The Italians tend to cook their vegetables more than other people – and certainly don't serve them almost raw as the French would. They need to be at the most *al dente*, or 'to the tooth'. To test, stick the tip of a sharp knife into the vegetable: if it offers resistance, cook a little longer; if there is little resistance, it should be ready. But ultimately it is all a matter of taste… **SERVES 4**

courgettes &
GREEN BEANS WITH MINT

In a large pan, cook the beans and courgettes in boiling salted water until *al dente*, probably about 15 minutes. Drain both and when still warm put in a bowl. Add the garlic, mint and oil, season with salt and pepper to taste and mix in the vinegar or lemon juice.

Leave at room temperature, uncovered, for at least half an hour to allow the vegetables absorb the flavours. The longer you leave them to infuse, the darker, softer and more garlicky they will become.

Serve with some good bread.

200g green (French) beans, trimmed
300g small courgettes, trimmed and quartered lengthways
salt and pepper
3 garlic cloves, peeled and roughly sliced
1 bunch fresh mint leaves
6 tbsp extra virgin olive oil
1 tbsp white wine vinegar or the juice of ½ lemon

LEFTOVERS

Any leftover courgettes or beans will be
delicious spread onto *crostini* (pieces
of toasted bread).

Roasted peppers, skinned and eaten as a salad, is one of my favourite pepper dishes. They are most delicious when prepared over a barbecue, but can also be cooked in the oven. You will find a recipe like this in *trattorias* from the middle of Italy right down to Sicily; it is a very southern dish. These peppers are great as an *antipasto*, but they can also be served with roast meats, and even with fish. **SERVES 4**

roasted
PEPPERS

Roast the peppers on a barbecue, turning them over frequently with tongs, until the skins are blackened and blistered. Depending on the flame, this can take quite a while. Don't be afraid of allowing them to become black; they're better overcooked than too raw – but you don't want them to turn to ash!

Alternatively, roast the peppers in a preheated oven at 200°C/Gas 6 for about 30–45 minutes. However, while this method is a little less labour-intensive, the flavour is not quite so good.

When the peppers are ready, put them in a dish to cool a little. I don't think they need to be put in a plastic bag or covered, despite the advice of many other chefs. When cool enough to handle, rub the skins off with your hands and discard, then slice the peppers in half and remove the stalks, inner membranes and seeds.

Cut the pepper flesh lengthways into narrow strips and place in a dish. Add the dressing ingredients and mix, seasoning with salt to taste. You can eat the dish straightaway, or leave it to become cold – but it is at its best the next day, when the flavours have had time to mingle.

4 firm and fleshy yellow and
   red sweet peppers

Dressing
2 garlic cloves, peeled and
   coarsely chopped
3 tbsp extra virgin olive oil
1 tbsp coarsely chopped
   flat-leaf parsley
salt

Some 25 years ago I invented the recipe for these little spinach balls for a chapter on finger food in a book published by the *Sunday Times*. Since then I have used them in all sorts of ways, most significantly in a vegetarian pasta dish (see page 58), and layered with pasta in a vegetarian *lasagne* (see page 62). They are very simple to make and very jolly. **MAKES 24 LITTLE BALLS**

spinach
BALLS

Wash the spinach, put it in a pan of salted boiling water and blanch for 2 minutes or so, then drain. Squeeze out as much water as you can, using your hands or pressing in a sieve, then chop the leaves finely.

Put the spinach in a medium bowl and stir in the beaten eggs, a pinch of salt, some pepper, the nutmeg, garlic, breadcrumbs and Parmesan. Mix well until you achieve a binding consistency. If the mixture is too wet, add an extra tablespoon of breadcrumbs.

Pour enough olive oil into a frying pan to cover the base generously, and heat gently.

Roll the mixture into little balls the size of walnuts. Shallow-fry the spinach balls in the hot olive oil until golden, about 4–5 minutes per side. Drain on kitchen paper and serve either warm or cold.

500g spinach, cleaned and
    tough stalks removed
salt and pepper
2 eggs, beaten
a pinch of freshly grated nutmeg
1 tsp very finely puréed garlic
100g fresh white breadcrumbs
50g Parmesan, freshly grated
olive oil, for shallow-frying

FRYING TIP

With any mixture to be shallow- or deep-fried, fry a little of it first, so that you can taste it for flavours and seasoning. If fine, carry on. If not, keep tinkering until you get it right.

Italians love preserved meat, particularly pork, which comes in all sorts of shapes, sizes and tastes. *Salami, prosciutto* and the exceptional dried and cured beef, *bresaola*, are often displayed on platters and accompanied by pickled vegetables like mushrooms, gherkins, onions and olives – which can all be bought in any good supermarket or Italian delicatessen. **PER PERSON (MULTIPLY AS NEEDED)**

air-dried
MEAT PLATTER

Display the meats 'artistically' on a platter, and bring through to the guests to help themselves. Usually *grissini* (crisp thin breadsticks), *crostini* (pieces of toasted bread) or unsalted crackers are eaten with the meats. It is important that they are unsalted because the preserved meats contain salt.

The most significant thing about this dish is that you don't need to cook at home, as everything is available from a good delicatessen.

a few slices each of Felino salami, Napoli salami and Calabrian hot sausage
a few slices of Parma ham, *bresaola* (beef) or *mortadella*
grissini, *crostini* or unsalted crackers

This recipe uses freshly boiled and mashed potato, but can also be made using leftover mashed potato. Canned tuna, preferably in olive oil, should always be at the ready in a well-stocked Italian larder. **MAKES 10 LITTLE CAKES**

potato &
TUNA CAKES

Cut the potatoes into walnut-sized pieces and boil in a large saucepan of salted water until soft, about 20 minutes. Drain well, then mash and leave to cool.

Put the mashed potato in a bowl. Add the tuna, capers, parsley and some pepper along with 2 of the eggs, and mix well.

Shape the mixture with your hands into cakes 8cm wide and 3cm deep. Beat the third egg in a bowl. Dip the cakes in the egg then coat with the breadcrumbs.

Pour enough olive oil into a frying pan to cover the base generously and heat gently.

Shallow-fry the cakes until golden, about 5 minutes per side. Drain on kitchen paper and serve either warm or cold.

550g potatoes
salt and pepper
250g canned tuna in oil, drained
    and finely chopped
30g salted capers, soaked
    (see page 24), drained
    and chopped
4 tbsp chopped flat-leaf parsley
3 eggs
about 100g dried breadcrumbs
olive oil, for shallow-frying

I like this combination of tomato and mozzarella without the usual basil, which I prefer to eat just with tomatoes. The rocket, particularly the wild variety, revives the rather bland tomato and mozzarella with its sharp taste. **SERVES 4**

rocket, tomato &
MOZZARELLA SALAD

To make the dressing, combine the oil, vinegar, sugar, salt and pepper in a small bowl and mix well.

Mix the rocket, tomatoes and mozzarella in a bowl and toss together with the dressing. Serve immediately (as the tomato becomes pulpy if left for too long).

100g rocket (preferably wild),
  cleaned and washed
200g tomatoes, quartered
150g buffalo mozzarella,
  cut into strips

Dressing
4 tbsp extra virgin olive oil
1 tbsp white wine vinegar
½ tsp caster sugar
salt and pepper

TO DE-SALT CAPERS

Salted capers are much better than vinegared ones (which never quite lose that vinegar flavour), but they have to be de-salted. Soak in cold water for about 15 minutes, spoon away any remaining salt and dry well.

I can't count the number of times I have surprised guests with this dish, which may be simple but holds plenty of flavour. If you are in a hurry you can buy a good mayonnaise, but it is much better (and not difficult) to make it yourself. You can do it! **SERVES 4–6**

tuna-stuffed
EGGS

Put the eggs in a small saucepan of cold water, bring to the boil and hard-boil for 15 minutes. Drain and leave to cool.

To make the mayonnaise, beat the egg yolks with a pinch of salt and the mustard in a bowl until creamy. Slowly pour in a little of the olive oil, whisking constantly until amalgamated. Keep adding the oil a little at a time, whisking all the while, until the mixture has thickened and all the oil has been used. Now add the lemon juice and mix well. Taste for seasoning and cover until needed.

Peel the eggs and cut in half. Remove the yolks, place in a bowl and, with a fork, reduce to a pulp. Mix this with the tuna, capers (reserving a few to use as garnish) and enough mayonnaise to be able to form balls the size of the original yolks. Place these in the holes of the halved egg whites.

Arrange the eggs in bowls, cover with some more mayonnaise and serve topped with the gherkin slices and reserved caper pieces.

6 large eggs
150g canned tuna in oil, drained
    and finely chopped
12 salted capers, soaked (see left),
    drained and finely chopped
1 gherkin (optional), finely sliced

Mayonnaise
2 egg yolks
salt and pepper
1 tsp French mustard
100ml olive oil (not extra virgin)
juice of ½ lemon

My favourite salads are the simplest ones, where the ingredients – and not too many of them – complement each other. The combination here of crisp gem lettuce and tender fennel bulb is extremely refreshing. **SERVES 4**

green salad
WITH FENNEL

Wash the lettuces and cut in quarters lengthways. Pull the leaves apart, discarding those on the outside if not tender. Put in a bowl. Discard the tougher outer leaves of the fennel, then cut the remaining flesh into very thin slices horizontally. Add to the bowl.

For the dressing, combine the oil, lemon juice and rind (or vinegar), salt and pepper in a small bowl and mix well. Pour over the salad, toss and serve.

4 baby gem lettuces
2 fennel bulbs
4 tbsp extra virgin olive oil
juice of ½ lemon, plus the finely
  grated rind, or, if you prefer,
  3 tbsp balsamic vinegar
salt and pepper

I tend not to use too much truffle oil because it is very intense, preferring to eat the real thing in season, but to counteract the slight bitterness of the chicory, the truffle oil is very good. This salad can be served as a starter, but also makes a wonderful side dish to roast beef or fillet steak. **SERVES 4**

belgian chicory salad
WITH TRUFFLE OIL

Trim off and discard the root ends of the chicory. Cut the white leaves into small strips and place in a bowl.

For the dressing, combine the olive oil, truffle oil, vinegar, a little salt and plenty of pepper in a small bowl and mix well. Pour into the bowl with the chicory and toss together. Serve topped with the summer truffle slices, if using.

4 heads Belgian chicory
30g summer truffle (optional),
    thinly sliced

Dressing
2 tbsp extra virgin olive oil
½ tsp truffle oil
2 tbsp balsamic vinegar
salt and pepper

I have long and fond memories of this salad. After the war, when I was in my mid-teens, my schoolmates and I were often very hungry in the afternoon. An impromptu afternoon snack of cabbage 'borrowed' from the local farmer, olive oil, vinegar and bread was easily organised! **SERVES 4**

savoy cabbage
SALAD

Remove the outer leaves of the cabbage until you are left with just the white centre. Slice this very thinly. Place the cabbage in a salad bowl.

Rub the slices of bread with the garlic clove.

For the dressing, combine the oil, vinegar, anchovies, a little salt and a lot of pepper in a small bowl and mix well. Pour into the bowl with the cabbage and toss. Eat with the garlic bread.

1 Savoy cabbage
4 large slices good country bread
1 garlic clove, peeled

Dressing
3 tbsp olive oil
1 tbsp white wine vinegar
2 anchovy fillets in oil,
   drained and very finely
   chopped
salt and pepper

My mother used to make this interesting dish for the sake of economy, but I make it because to me it tastes of summer – and none go by without me making it a few times at least. She used stale bread, which was baked in the oven to make it more absorbent and edible. **SERVES 4**

bread & vegetable
SALAD

Preheat the oven to 160°C/Gas 3, and bake the bread for about 20 minutes, until golden. Break the cooked bread into small pieces about the size of a large sugar lump.

Put the tomatoes into a bowl of water that has just come to the boil, and leave for 30 seconds. Pull off the skin, then chop the flesh coarsely, collecting all the juices. (If your tomatoes are not very juicy, you'll need some help with soaking the bread, try adding some tomato juice from a carton or can.)

Mix the tomato pieces and juices together with all the other ingredients, including the bread. Leave to infuse for a few hours, so that the bread can absorb all the flavours and soften. Stir occasionally. Add salt and pepper to taste and serve cold.

4 large slices country bread, crusts removed
4 large ripe tomatoes (about 800g)
the tender centre of 1 head celery, plus leaves, coarsely chopped
10 basil leaves, chopped
10 pitted olives, green or black
1 bunch spring onions, chopped
1 yellow pepper, seeded and cut into fine strips
1 garlic clove (optional), peeled and puréed
6 tbsp extra virgin olive oil
salt and pepper

I can't stress enough that you must buy very fresh, small beetroot for this salad – ready-cooked will not do. I usually get mine in season from my garden, and they are a delicacy. The combination of fresh mint and sweet beetroot make an excellent dish that is not only a great starter but also a wonderful accompaniment to roast chicken or grilled fish. **SERVES 4**

beetroot salad
WITH MINT

Cook the beetroot in plenty of boiling water until the tip of a knife enters the beetroot very easily (about 30 minutes). Drain well.

When cool enough to handle, peel the beetroot and cut into thin slices. Put in a bowl and add the mint.

For the dressing, combine the oil, vinegar, salt and pepper in a small bowl and mix well. Toss together with the beetroot slices and mint and serve.

16 small fresh beetroot
20 mint leaves

Dressing
4 tbsp extra virgin olive oil
1 tbsp white wine vinegar
salt and pepper

soups

For this soup, the ingredients are raw, and the mixture of the two soups and two colours is spectacular to look at. It is a delightfully refreshing dish for a hot summer's day! **SERVES 4**

raw cucumber &
TOMATO SUMMER SOUP

Liquidise the cucumber with the dill in a liquidiser or food processor. Add the cream and season to taste with a little salt and pepper. Leave to chill in the fridge.

Liquidise the skinned tomatoes with the basil and onion. Season to taste with salt and pepper and chill in the fridge.

To serve, first put the cucumber soup in a deep soup bowl, then carefully add the tomato soup in the centre and garnish with a few basil leaves. For extra colour and texture, try adding a tablespoon of very finely chopped mixed tomato and cucumber to each serving.

1 large cucumber, peeled
   and cut into chunks
2 tbsp finely chopped dill
3 tbsp double cream
salt and pepper
2 large beef tomatoes, skinned
   and chopped
10 basil leaves, plus extra
   to garnish
1 white onion, peeled and
   roughly chopped

As with *minestrone* this pasta and bean soup exists in at least 20 versions, depending on the region where it originates. It is usually based on a stock flavoured by a Parma ham bone: though vegetarian versions, such as this one below, are now rather fashionable. **SERVES 6**

pasta &
BEAN SOUP

If you are using dried beans, soak in water overnight, boil in unsalted water for 2–3 hours until tender, and drain.

Fry the celery in the olive oil in a large saucepan over a medium heat for a few minutes before adding the chilli.

After about 10 minutes add the garlic and cook for a couple of minutes, until soft, then add the tomatoes. Wait a further 10 minutes before adding two-thirds of the beans, keeping the remainder aside to be mashed and added to thicken the dish.

Pour in the stock or water and bring to the boil. Now add the pasta and, after 8 minutes add the basil leaves and the mashed beans. Season to taste with salt and pepper and serve.

250g dried borlotti or cannellini
    beans, or 3 x 400g cans
    unsalted borlotti beans,
    drained and rinsed
2 celery stalks, cubed
4 tbsp extra virgin olive oil
1 fresh red chilli, chopped
2 garlic cloves, peeled and
    finely chopped
3 ripe tomatoes, skinned
    and chopped, or 400g canned
    chopped tomatoes
1 litre vegetable stock or water
115g mixed small pasta pieces
    or *tubettini*
10 basil leaves, shredded
salt and pepper

The word *velouté* is borrowed from the French, which means a soup with a velvety consistency. *Passata* would be more Italian but since the French borrow Italian culinary terminology, why not the reverse? The cep or *porcino* is the king of wild mushrooms, and is available fresh only during its brief season. **SERVES 4**

cep & cannellini
BEAN VELOUTÉ

Soak the dried cannellini beans in water overnight. Drain, then add the beans to a large saucepan, cover with fresh water, bring to the boil and cook for 10 minutes. Reduce the heat to a simmer and cook for a further 1½–2 hours. Drain.

Clean the porcini carefully, brushing off any dust, and checking inside the stems for any unwelcome visitors. Cut the mushrooms and stems into slices. Sauté the porcini in the butter with the garlic clove for 10 minutes. Remove the garlic from the pan and discard, then season to taste with salt and pepper.

Put the stock in a pan, add the cannellini beans and porcini and cook for a few minutes. Season, then add the double cream and liquidise in a food processor to obtain a velvety consistency. Pour into serving bowls and, sprinkle with Parmesan, if desired.

150g dried cannellini beans
400g small fresh porcini (ceps)
60g butter
1 whole garlic clove, peeled
salt and pepper
500ml vegetable stock
40ml double cream
50g Parmesan (optional),
   freshly grated

Autumn and winter offer lots of roots and squash which can be used in soup. This type of pumpkin soup is more likely to be served in the north and especially the northeast part of Italy, from where *speck* (an air-dried and smoked shoulder of pork) originates. **SERVES 4**

pumpkin
SOUP

Fry the onion in 2 tbsp of the olive oil in a large saucepan until soft, but not browning, about 10 minutes.

Add the stock and, when boiling, the cubes of pumpkin and celeriac, and cook until soft, about 15–20 minutes. Add salt and pepper to taste. Liquidise in a food processor or blender and return to the pan to reheat gently.

Meanwhile, heat the remaining oil in a frying pan. Add the *speck* or *pancetta* and cook until crisp. Add the rosemary and stir to combine. Set aside.

Pour the warmed soup into serving bowls and top with the *speck* or *pancetta* and rosemary mixture. Serve hot.

1 onion, peeled and
    finely chopped
6 tbsp olive oil
1 litre chicken or vegetable stock
600g pumpkin flesh, cut
    into cubes
200g celeriac, peeled and cut
    into cubes
salt and pepper
a thick slice of *speck* or *pancetta*,
    about 60g, cut into cubes
a few rosemary needles

In Italy there are as many recipes for *minestrone* ('big *minestra*' as soups are called when based on vegetables and greens) as there are households. Depending on what is in season, or what is in the house, a *minestrone* can vary a lot, though usually it includes some beans, potatoes, tomatoes, cabbage, spinach, cauliflower, carrots, with herb flavours like basil, rosemary and even pesto. **SERVES 4**

thick vegetable
SOUP

Fry the onion in the olive oil in a large pan for about 5 minutes, then add all the diced vegetables and the beans or chickpeas. Cover with stock or water, crumble in the stock cubes, cover with the lid and leave to gently simmer for 30 minutes, until the vegetables are soft.

Add the basil and season to taste. Sprinkle with Parmesan, if desired, drizzle with extra virgin olive oil and serve.

1 large onion, peeled and diced
6 tbsp olive oil
150g each of carrots and
    potatoes, peeled and diced
150g each of courgettes, celery
    and tomatoes, diced
150g fresh podded borlotti beans
    or peas, or cooked chickpeas
1.5 litres vegetable stock or water
2 vegetable stock cubes
10 basil leaves, shredded
salt and pepper
50g Parmesan (optional),
    freshly grated
extra virgin olive oil

I tend to eat this simple dish anywhere I can find it. The little stuffed pasta – *tortellini*, *cappelletti*, or *anolini* as they call them in Bologna – are usually hand-made, and look amazing. Although I think they look like little hats, some imaginative Italians have christened them 'Venus's belly button'. While preparing them from fresh is quite difficult, you can buy a ready-made fresh variety from good delicatessens. **SERVES 4**

stuffed pasta
IN BROTH

Put the stock into a pan, and boil gently until it has reduced to 600ml. This intensifies the flavour.

Bring the stock back to the boil and check for salt and pepper. Add the pasta and cook according to the instructions of the vendor or the packet, usually between 4–6 minutes (but it can vary a lot).

Spoon the stock and pasta into deep soup plates and sprinkle over the grated Parmesan to finish.

1 litre chicken or beef stock
salt and pepper
400g good-quality fresh *tortellini*
  or *cappelletti*
60g Parmesan, freshly grated

Fish soups are very regional, being made differently, often from village to village, along the coastline of Italy. In the Marche region it is called *brodetto*, 'little broth', and uses the local fresh fish. A fish soup is also classic in Venice, which incorporates various molluscs from the lagoon. **SERVES 4**

simple
FISH SOUP

First of all heat the olive oil in a large saucepan and fry the onion until softened, about 6–7 minutes. Add the *passata*, and in this cook the mussels, monkfish and squid rings, for about 10 minutes. Discard any mussels that haven't opened.

Stir in your fish soup and heat through gently, about 5 minutes. Placing a slice of toasted bread at the base of each, pour the soup into bowls and serve.

6 tbsp olive oil
1 small onion, peeled and
    finely chopped
2–3 tbsp *passata*
1kg mussels, cleaned
300g monkfish, cut into
    medium cubes
300g squid, cleaned and cut
    into rings
at least 500ml good French
    soupe de poissons (in most
    supermarkets or delicatessens)
4 thick slices country bread,
    toasted

pasta

TYPES OF PASTA

Most commercial pasta is made with durum (hard) wheat semolina and water. It is extruded through a machine with a die at high pressure, cut to size and then dried in a process lasting some 12 hours. Other commercial, dried pastas are made with the addition of eggs. This gives more protein and a different texture.

There is also a hand-made pasta, made with just water, durum wheat semolina and 00 flour. This comes usually from Puglia where they hand-make *orrecchiette*, *fusilli*, *strozzapreti* and *cecatelli*, and also from Tuscany, where the pasta is called *strangozzi*.

Stuffed pastas are also available everywhere now, such as *ravioli*, *tortellini*, *tortelloni*, *tortelli* and *cappelletti* (very good in broth). These are best freshly made, and can be bought in good delicatessens.

For special occasions, Italians feel they must make their own fresh pasta, either simply with flour and water, or with egg. In my opinion there are very few good fresh pastas available in shops, and I firmly believe the best is one that you make yourself. If you do want to try it, see page 107 for a recipe for fresh *fusilli*.

PASTA SAUCES

Right pasta, right sauce

Spaghetti and all round and long pastas are suitable for most sauces, but not *bolognese*. The ideal pastas for *bolognese* are home-made egg *tagliatelle* (a flat ribbon of pasta), and dried egg and egg-less *tagliatelle* (from shops). *Tagliolini*, the smallest form of *tagliatelle*, is particularly good with truffle and other delicate sauces like crab or lobster. Angel's hair or *capelli d'angelo* is a particularly thin type of long pasta, which is wonderful with a simple tomato sauce and even in broth. Short bulky pasta like *paccheri*, *macaroni* and *penne* are good for *arrabbiata* or long-cooked meat and tomato *ragù*. The very small pasta, *pastina*, is used in broth and soups.

Tomato pasta sauces

The majority of Italian pasta sauces contain tomatoes. Besides colour, a ripe tomato gives a certain degree of acidity to balance the other ingredients, which results in a wonderful taste. Out of season (and sometimes in season too), Italians now use a great deal of canned and jarred tomato products, which are very convenient indeed.

CANNED PEELED TOMATOES, called *pelati*, which contain the seeds, pulp and lots of water, can be used in long-cooking sauces.

CHOPPED TOMATOES IN CANS, also called tomato pulp are very useful. The pulp is in chunks, without seeds or skin, and can be used for any sort of sauce.

TOMATO PASSATA in jars is liquidised and strained tomato, which is of a thinnish consistency (often too thin for my liking). This can be used by itself (as a sort of coulis) or in combination with the other two above for long-cooking sauces, and also for immediate use.

TOMATO CONCENTRATE is a paste or purée (usually in a tube, sometimes a little can), which consists of a double concentration of tomato. This is used to reinforce the taste of normal tomatoes. In Sicily they use a six-times concentrate sold everywhere called *strattu*, from 'extract'. It is solid, very dark in colour and has to be diluted with water.

Other pasta sauces

MEATS are often used in sauces. Minced beef, veal, pork or even game like wild boar, deer, hare and pheasant, etc., are used for *ragù* (long-cooked sauces). Sometimes chicken livers and sweetbreads are added. Cured and preserved meats (*speck*, smoked ham, *pancetta*, Parma ham, *salami*) are also great flavour additions.

ALL TYPES OF SEAFOOD, like mussels, clams, lobster, crab, scallops, prawns, shrimps, cuttlefish, squid, octopus, and many de-boned fish such as red mullet, monkfish, sardines, tuna and even Dover sole, are used in a number of popular pasta sauces. Canned or jarred anchovies, either preserved in salt or oil, are particularly important.

VEGETABLES such as broccoli, cauliflower, chicory, green beans, broad beans, peas, artichokes, asparagus, borlotti and cannellini beans, potatoes, spinach, pumpkin, beetroot, chickpeas and mushrooms add texture and flavour to pasta sauces. Onion and garlic (sometimes together) are basics, as are carrot and celery (all forming part of what the Italians call *soffritto*). Dried porcini mushrooms (ceps) are wonderful when the fresh are not available.

FLAVOURINGS AND CONDIMENTS vary enormously. Olive oil, butter or both together, are vital, as are salt and pepper, eggs on occasion, and truffle oil every now and then. I'm not fond of cream with pasta unless I am making *tortellini* with cream and ham, as I find it reduces everything to the same taste. Wine and vinegar play a part, as do the great cheeses of Italy – Parmesan and grana padano, Fontina, Gorgonzola, pecorino, mozzarella and Taleggio.

A lack of success in pasta sauces is often due to the wrong use of herbs. Italians don't use them too profligately, just appropriately to the dish. Celery leaves, basil, parsley (flat-leaf), chives, chervil, rosemary, fresh oregano (very strong), mint, rocket and chillies are used often, but with care and love.

Whatever you choose, do remember that in Italy generally the simpler the better.

PASTA COOKING AND EATING

• The pot for boiling the pasta must be high and large.

• Use 1 litre of water for 100g pasta.

• For small portions, allow 50g of pasta per person; 70–80g for normal portions and 100–110g for large portions.

• Add 10g salt per litre to the water just before boiling.

• Place the pasta into the boiling water and stir after 20–30 seconds.

• Don't add oil unless you are cooking pasta sheets like *lasagne*.

• Cook from 2–3 minutes for fresh home-made pasta and up to 18–20 minutes for dried non-egg pasta (follow the directions on the packet).

• For soups or minestrones put the pasta directly in the stock.

• Test one piece of pasta towards the end of cooking to see if it is to your liking. The Italians like it cooked, but still with a light resistance to the tooth (*al dente*).

• Have the sauce prepared, and place a few tablespoons in a hot soup bowl.

• Drain the pasta, but do not wash under cold water, and mix with a little of the sauce. (The sauce might benefit from a few tablespoons of the pasta cooking water if it is too thick.)

• Place portions in hot plates, and top up with more sauce. But remember, the pasta mustn't be swimming in the sauce.

• If necessary add freshly grated Parmesan or pecorino cheese. Pasta with fish sauce is better tossed with the sauce in the pan (and no Parmesan added).

• Serve the pasta hot, and if it is long, eat only with a fork: lift a few strings of pasta from the plate, make a little space on the side, pin the fork down and start to twirl. This is to avoid too big a morsel. Try also not to suck strings into your mouth (although this is permitted for babies). Eat only soupy pasta with a spoon. This is the be-all and end-all of pasta etiquette!

This is probably one of the most popular recipes for native Italians. They like to eat it at any time, but it's probably the prime dish to be eaten for a midnight feast, when they arrive home late and hungry. It takes only about 6–7 minutes to cook the pasta, while the 'sauce' is ready in less than half that time. You don't even have to grate any Parmesan, as the pasta is better without it.

SERVES 2 (MULTIPLY AS NEEDED)

spaghetti with
GARLIC, OIL & CHILLI

Put plenty of water in a saucepan, add salt, bring to the boil and throw in the pasta. Stir, then cook for about 5–6 minutes, until nearly done.

Now start the sauce by heating the olive oil gently in a deep frying pan. Add the garlic and chilli and fry for a few seconds, or until the garlic starts to change colour. Take care not to burn the garlic.

The pasta will be ready and *al dente* in those few minutes. Drain it well and put in the pan with the 'sauce', adding a little salt and perhaps 1–2 tbsp of the pasta cooking water. Stir a couple of times and serve.

salt
180g *spaghetti*

Sauce
2 garlic cloves, peeled and
   finely chopped
1 small red chilli, finely chopped
6 tbsp olive oil

This pesto recipe, which comes from Liguria in the north, is cooked with various types of pasta like *trenette* (similar to *linguine*), *manilli de sea* (flat home-made pasta like sheets of *lasagne*), or with gnocchi. Here I have suggested using *trofie*, a pasta that is shaped in little twisted pieces. **SERVES 4**

pasta
WITH PESTO

Cook the pasta in plenty of boiling salted water in a large saucepan until *al dente*, about 8–9 minutes. When ready, drain well, reserving some of the pasta cooking water.

For the sauce, remove the stalks from the basil, chop the leaves roughly and put in a blender. Add the garlic, pine kernels and a large pinch of salt and blend, adding the olive oil in a stream as you do. When you see the mixture is still slightly coarse (after a few seconds), add the cheese and some more oil, just enough oil to obtain a moist mixture.

Pour the pesto into a pan and warm gently. Throw in the drained pasta, add about 4 tbsp of the pasta cooking water and mix well. Serve at once, with a little more grated cheese, if you like.

320g dried *trofie*
salt

Pesto sauce
1 bunch basil leaves
1 garlic clove, peeled and
    finely chopped
30g pine kernels
salt
about 50ml olive oil
60g pecorino cheese or
    Parmesan, freshly grated

Ready in a few minutes, this simple tomato sauce is a perfect dish for feeding one in a hurry. It is made with *pomodorini* (cherry tomatoes) – though it works with very ripe chopped ordinary tomatoes or canned chopped tomatoes as well. I deliberately don't add Parmesan to this dish because I like the pure taste and simplicity of the tomatoes; should you desire it, grate a little over the top before serving. **SERVES 1 (MULTIPLY AS NEEDED)**

thin spaghetti
WITH TOMATO & BASIL

For the sauce, fry the garlic in the oil until soft but not brown, about 2 minutes. Add the tomatoes and basil and cook for a few more minutes. Season if needed.

Cook the pasta in plenty of boiling salted water in a large saucepan until *al dente*, about 5–6 minutes, before draining. Add to the sauce, mix well and serve, drizzled with a little extra virgin olive oil.

100g *spaghettini*
salt and pepper
extra virgin olive oil

Sauce
1 garlic clove, peeled and sliced
2 tbsp olive oil
100g *pomodorini*, chopped
5 basil leaves, shredded

I was brought up with truffles, not because my family was rich but because my father was a friend of a *trifolau*, someone who searches with their dogs for the precious fungus (I now have my own, the very special Sandrino, in Asti). When, very rarely, we had a truffle, my mother would make fresh egg *tagliolini*, the thinnest type of flat *tagliatelle*. This recipe approximates the taste of that dish, without reflecting its hefty price tag! **SERVES 4**

pasta with
TRUFFLE BUTTER

Cook the pasta in a large saucepan of plenty of boiling salted water until *al dente*: for fresh pasta about 2–4 minutes; for dried pasta, follow the instructions on the packet. When ready, drain, reserving 6 tbsp of the pasta cooking water.

Put the butter in a pan and melt, then add the reserved pasta cooking water for moisture. Add the drained pasta and Parmesan and toss well to combine. Serve hot.

400g fresh or dried egg *tagliolini*
salt

Sauce
100g truffle butter
   (available in good delicatessens)
60g Parmesan, freshly grated

This is probably the cheapest dish in the book, but it is also extremely easy to make and very enjoyable. It originates from the Tyrolean part of Italy, bordering with Austria, where you may find various dishes that are 'left over' from the years of the Austro-Hungarian Empire. I was in Vienna for New Year's Eve in 2008, and had the pleasure of eating this simplest of dishes. It can be cooked with olive oil but I prefer lard, in which case it is obviously not vegetarian any more. **SERVES 4**

cabbage &
ONION PASTA

To make the sauce, heat the olive oil or lard in a large saucepan, and add the onion. Cook gently until soft, about 6–7 minutes. Add the cabbage and the water, put the lid on and cook gently for a further 20–30 minutes, until the cabbage is soft.

Take the lid off the pan, and add the sugar. Cook gently until it has melted, stirring constantly. It will caramelise and begin to brown. Add a little salt and the vinegar. The mixture should be dry.

In a saucepan of boiling salted water, cook the pasta until *al dente*, probably about 10 minutes, but follow the instructions on the packet. Drain well.

Mix the pasta and sauce together and serve with plenty of pepper.

salt and pepper
250g large dried egg *tagliatelle*,
    broken into small pieces

Sauce
8 tbsp olive oil or 60g lard
200g white onion, peeled and
    finely chopped
600g white cabbage, cut into
    small chunks
150ml water
50g caster sugar
a few drops of white wine vinegar

This is a recipe I created for Carluccio's Caffés. It is still on the menu, and every time someone orders it, some money goes to charity. It has proved so popular that Carluccio's was able to collect £70,000 in just three months! **SERVES 4**

pasta with courgettes
& SPINACH BALLS

Prepare the spinach balls in advance and keep them warm in a very low oven.

In a saucepan of boiling salted water, cook the pasta until *al dente*, about 8–10 minutes. When ready, drain, reserving a few tablespoons of the pasta cooking water.

Meanwhile, make the sauce. Fry the garlic and chilli in the oil for about a minute – don't let the garlic brown – then add the courgettes, and cook for 3–4 minutes, until the courgettes have started to soften.

Add the Parmesan to the sauce, season to taste and mix well, then toss thoroughly with the drained pasta and reserved cooking water. Serve hot with the warmed spinach balls on top.

1 recipe spinach balls
(see page 18)
400g *rigatoni* (large ridged
pasta tubes)
salt and pepper

Sauce
2 garlic cloves, peeled and
finely chopped
1 chilli, finely chopped
8 tbsp olive oil
2 courgettes, trimmed and
finely grated
60g Parmesan, freshly grated

Frittedda, in the Sicilian dialect, means a stew of asparagus, young onions, small broad beans, peas and artichokes, all of which are in season between March and April. It makes an excellent sauce for the largest size of pasta ribbon, *pappardelle*. **SERVES 4–6**

wide pasta ribbons
WITH SPRINGTIME SAUCE

To make the sauce, first prepare the artichokes by removing the tough outer leaves and trim the base of the stems. With a sharp knife, trim the tips of the leaves, leaving only the tender parts. Cut into quarters and remove any choke.

Put all the vegetables in a large saucepan with the oil and water. Cook gently for 20 minutes then, when you are sure everything is cooked, add some salt and pepper and the parsley. Mix well.

In a saucepan of boiling salted water, cook the pasta until *al dente*, about 7–8 minutes. Drain and mix with the sauce. Sprinkle with Parmesan cheese, if desired, and serve.

350g *pappardelle*
salt and pepper
freshly grated Parmesan
   (optional)

Sauce
8 small artichokes
300g asparagus
300g white young onions, peeled
   and finely sliced
300g podded tender broad beans
200g podded tender garden peas
6 tbsp olive oil
100ml water
3 tbsp coarsely chopped parsley

Not long ago I had the enviable task of cooking a famous timbale for a BBC TV documentary about the Sicilian Principe di Salina, Tomasi di Lampedusa (*Il Gattopardo* or The Leopard). The historical recipe turned out to be a triumph, but was a little too elaborate for this book. So I have devised this pasta dish instead, which requires a little bit of work and should probably be made for celebrations and special occasions. To make life simpler you can prepare it the day before serving. **SERVES 8–10**

rich oven-baked
VEGETABLE PASTA

Make the tomato sauce first by frying the onion in the olive oil until soft, about 5–6 minutes. Add the tomato and basil and cook gently for 20–30 minutes. Season with salt and set aside.

For the filling, dust the aubergine and courgette slices with flour. Beat 4 of the eggs together, and dip the vegetable slices in this. Pour enough olive oil into a large frying pan to cover the base generously and heat gently. Shallow-fry the vegetable slices a few at a time until golden, about 3–4 minutes on each side. Set both vegetables and oil aside. If you haven't cooked them in advance, the spinach balls can also be cooked in this oil.

600g large *rigatoni*
salt and pepper

Tomato sauce
2 large onions, peeled and
   finely chopped
100ml olive oil
1.5kg tomato pulp (*polpa di
   pomodoro*) or canned
   chopped tomatoes
10 basil leaves, shredded

Meanwhile, boil the baby courgettes and the fennel bulbs in a pan of lightly salted water until *al dente*, about 6–7 minutes. Drain well and cut the fennel into slices.

Now cook the pasta in plenty of boiling salted water until *al dente*, about 5–6 minutes. Drain and mix with little of the sauce. Preheat the oven to 200°C/Gas 6.

In a baking tray or dish, now assemble all the ingredients. First put a layer of pasta on the base on which you distribute slices of aubergine and courgette, slices of fennel, the whole baby courgettes and a few spinach balls. Sprinkle over some of the cheese chunks, some of the tomato sauce and some of the grated Parmesan. Build a few layers according to the size of the baking tray, and finish on top with tomato sauce, a few little chunks of the melting cheese, a few spinach balls, and the remaining Parmesan.

Bake for 30–40 minutes in the preheated oven. Let it rest for 10–15 minutes before serving, cut in squares. Wonderful…

Filling
2 aubergines, cut in 8mm thick
   slices lengthways
2 courgettes, cut in 8mm thick
   slices lengthways
plain flour, to dust
6 eggs
olive oil, for shallow-frying
1 recipe spinach balls
   (see page 18)
8 whole baby courgettes,
   trimmed
2 fennel bulbs, trimmed
600g melting cheese, like Fontina,
   Bel Paese, Taleggio, cut into
   little chunks
200g Parmesan, freshly grated

When I mention *funghi* I tend to mean porcini or ceps, usually fresh. However, it is possible to achieve good results either with a mixture of *funghi*, like chanterelles, oysters and field mushrooms, plus some dried porcini for that unmistakeable mushroom taste. *Tagliatelle* may be egg pasta – either fresh (which is best home-made) or dried – or it could just be simple *tagliatelle* with no eggs. **SERVES 4**

mushroom
NOODLES

For the sauce, heat the olive oil in a large pan and fry the onion and garlic until beginning to soften, about 6 minutes. After a few minutes add the fresh mushrooms and sauté for 10–15 minutes. Add the chopped porcini and a little of their soaking water for moisture. Stir in the butter and parsley and season to taste.

Cook the pasta in plenty of boiling salted water until *al dente*, about 6–7 minutes. Drain and mix well with the sauce. Serve on hot plates with the Parmesan sprinkled on top.

400g *tagliatelle*
salt and pepper
60g Parmesan, freshly grated

Sauce
6 tbsp olive oil
1 large onion, peeled and
    finely chopped
1 garlic clove, peeled and
    finely chopped
400g mixed fresh mushrooms,
    cleaned and sliced
50g dried porcini (ceps),
    rehydrated and chopped
50g unsalted butter
2 tbsp finely chopped
    flat-leaf parsley

The Sardinians, during their centuries of isolation due to so many invasions, lived mainly inland. As a result, they acquired more of a taste for meat and game. Many different types of pasta and breads are also unique to the island. *Gnocchetti sardi* or *malloreddus* as they call them, meaning 'little bulls', is a delightful pasta, ideally cooked with tomato-based meaty sauces. You can buy it in packets in good delicatessens. **SERVES 4–6**

sardinian pasta
WITH LAMB SAUCE

For the sauce, heat the olive oil in a pan, add the onion and fry gently to soften, about 6–7 minutes, then add the meat and stir to brown on all sides. Add the wine and heat to allow the alcohol to evaporate for a few minutes. Add the tomato and herbs, cover and stew slowly on top of the stove for 2–3 hours. Check from time to time, and add a little water if it seems too thick.

Remove the meat from the juices and discard the bones. Cut or flake the meat in smaller pieces and return to the sauce. Season with salt and pepper to taste, and if extra moisture is still needed, add 2–3 tbsp pasta cooking water.

Cook the pasta in plenty of boiling salted water until *al dente*, probably about 8–9 minutes. Drain and put in a large bowl with half of the sauce. Mix well, divide between the plates and top with a little more sauce and the grated pecorino.

400g *gnocchetti sardi*
salt and pepper
80g aged pecorino cheese, grated

Sauce
5 tbsp olive oil
1 large onion, peeled and
    finely chopped
600g lamb on the bone, or slices
    of the lower part of the leg
    (*ossobuco*)
100ml dry white wine
enough tomato pulp (*polpa di
    pomodoro*) to cover the meat,
    or canned chopped tomatoes
2–3 bay leaves
a few rosemary needles

When you buy a chicken in Italy, it still contains (as it does if you buy from a good butcher) the tasty and very useful giblets. Comprising the liver, gizzard, heart and sometimes neck, they can make a great pasta sauce. **SERVES 4**

egg noodles with
CHICKEN GIBLETS

For the sauce, cut the gizzard into thin slices, and the liver and heart into smaller pieces. Leave the neck whole; it's for flavouring.

Fry the onion in the oil until soft, about 5–6 minutes, then add the giblets and cook, stirring, for 5 minutes. Add the porcini and fry for a few more minutes. Add the wine, cook for a further minute, season, then add a little of the mushroom soaking water until you have a sauce-like consistency.

Cook the pasta in plenty of boiling salted water until *al dente*, usually about 3 minutes if fresh or 4–5 minutes if dried. Drain the pasta, reserving a little of the pasta cooking water.

Add the butter to the sauce, warm up and use to dress the pasta. Should the sauce need any liquid, add 2 tbsp of the reserved pasta water. Divide between the plates, sprinkle over the grated Parmesan and serve.

400g fresh or dried egg *tagliolini*
salt and pepper
60g Parmesan, freshly grated

Sauce
300g chicken giblets
1 large onion, peeled and
    finely chopped
4 tbsp olive oil
30g dried porcini (ceps),
    rehydrated and finely chopped
4 tbsp white wine
30g unsalted butter

This is a Venetian speciality, and is very easy to make. In the Veneto, people still make the special pasta by hand with the help of a little implement – a *torcolo* – which has a chamber through which the pasta is pushed. This produces a thick *spaghetti* with a 4mm diameter and no hole. The alternative is *bucatini*, which is the same size, but has a little hole inside. **SERVES 4**

spaghetti with onion
& ANCHOVY SAUCE

For the sauce, fry the onions in a pan with the olive oil until soft, about 6–7 minutes, then add the anchovies, which will dissolve in the heat. Stir them in very briefly.

Cook the pasta in plenty of boiling salted water until *al dente*, probably about 8–9 minutes. Drain and mix into the sauce. Season with a little salt and plenty of pepper. Mix well and serve hot.

400g *bigoli* or *bucatini*
salt and pepper

Sauce
600g onions, peeled and
   finely chopped
6 tbsp olive oil
40g anchovy fillets in oil

This recipe goes back to the time when the agricultural people from the country drove into town in carts pulled by horses and donkeys. The driver knew how to cook something unusual and extremely tasty for himself when he reached his destination. **SERVES 2 (CAN BE MULTIPLIED)**

cart-driver
SPAGHETTI

For the sauce, fry the onion in a pan with the olive oil until soft, about 5–6 minutes, then add the tomatoes and fry for 15 minutes. Add the sliced porcini and some of their liquid, along with the tuna and some salt and pepper to taste.

Cook the pasta in plenty of boiling salted water until *al dente*, about 5–6 minutes. Drain, mix with the sauce and serve immediately.

200g *spaghetti*
salt and pepper

Sauce
1 small onion, peeled and
    finely sliced
4 tbsp olive oil
2 ripe tomatoes, finely chopped
25g dried porcini (ceps),
    rehydrated and finely sliced
100g canned tuna in oil, drained

I had the good fortune in Italy to find small black *spaghettini*, almost as fine as angel's hair. This type of pasta is made by incorporating the black ink of cuttlefish, and is very typical of Venice. If you can't find this pasta, you can substitute black *tagliatelle*. The other alternative is to buy normal *spaghettini* and add the black ink (which is fairly readily available in good delicatessens) to the sauce. **SERVES 4**

spaghettini with
SCALLOPS & SHRIMPS

While you cook the pasta in plenty of boiling salted water as usual, until *al dente*, about 4–5 minutes, you have time to make the sauce.

Put the olive oil, garlic and chilli in a large frying pan and fry briefly until the garlic has softened. Add the scallops, shrimps and wine, and fry for a further 2 minutes. Add the parsley, salt and pepper to taste, and the sauce is ready.

Drain the pasta, add to the sauce, mix well and divide between the plates, finishing each with a drizzle of extra virgin olive oil.

400g black *spaghettini* or
  tagliatelle
salt and pepper
a little extra virgin olive oil

Sauce
4 tbsp olive oil
2 garlic cloves, peeled and
  finely chopped
1 small red chilli, finely chopped
8 large shelled scallops
  with corals
200g cooked pink shrimps,
  shelled
50ml dry white wine
2 tbsp coarsely chopped
  flat-leaf parsley

You will find this dish in all the coastal towns and villages, most famously in the laguna of Venice. It is the seafood pasta 'par excellence'. There exist two versions of the sauce: in *rosso* (with tomatoes) or in *bianco* (without tomatoes). I prefer the second, featured here, as you can appreciate the taste of the seafood much more easily. **SERVES 4**

linguine with clams
& MUSSELS

For the sauce, put the mussels and clams in a large saucepan with the olive oil, wine, garlic and chilli (if using). Bring to the boil with the lid on and cook for a further 10 minutes before removing from the heat. Discard any mussels that haven't opened. Remove the meat from the shells (reserving a few for garnish) and keep to one side. Discard the empty shells.

At the base of the pan will be the sauce made of oil, wine, juices from the shells, garlic and chilli, if desired. Keep this warm.

In a separate pan, cook the pasta in plenty of boiling salted water until *al dente*, about 6–7 minutes. Drain and add to the sauce. Add salt, lots of pepper and the parsley, along with the shellfish flesh.

Divide between the plates, adding a few drops of extra virgin olive oil and the few remaining shell-on fish. Serve immediately.

400g *linguine*
salt and pepper
1 bunch flat-leaf parsley,
    finely chopped
extra virgin olive oil

Sauce
1kg mussels, cleaned
1kg small clams, cleaned
6 tbsp olive oil
100ml dry white wine
2 garlic cloves, peeled and
    finely diced
1 small red chilli (optional),
    chopped

This is a typical Pugliese coastal dish, from Bari, which was originally accompanied by what is known as *cime di rape*, or rape tops. These are not generally available outside Italy, and the easiest alternative is little tips of broccoli (the calabrese type) or purple sprouting broccoli. Instead of *orecchiette* you could try this recipe with *gnocchetti sardi* or *penne*. **SERVES 4–6**

ear-shaped pasta with
BROCCOLI & MUSSELS

For the sauce, boil the florets in a saucepan of salted water until *al dente*, about 8–9 minutes. Drain.

Using a large frying pan with a lid, add the olive oil, garlic, chilli and tomatoes. Fry briefly, until the garlic has softened, then add the mussels and cover with the lid. Continue to cook until the mussels have opened, about 10 minutes. Discard any that have not opened, and most of the shells, saving the mussel meat in the sauce.

Add the cooked broccoli florets and heat up to allow the broccoli to absorb the flavours.

Cook the pasta in plenty of boiling salted water until *al dente*, about 10–12 minutes. Drain well and mix with the sauce. Season with a little salt and lots of pepper and serve in deep plates.

350g *orecchiette pugliesi*
salt and pepper

Sauce
300g small broccoli florets
6 tbsp olive oil
2 garlic cloves, peeled and
    finely sliced
1 small chilli, chopped
200g cherry tomatoes, halved
800g mussels, cleaned

gnocchi, polenta
& RICE

GNOCCHI

A variety of gnocchi exist, but the simplest and most widely encountered are those made with mashed potatoes and a little flour. To make them is simplicity itself. For a serving for four people, cook and mash 400g of floury potatoes, then mix with 100g of plain flour and an egg. Using your hands, roll a little of this mixture at a time into sausage shapes. Cut these into 3cm chunks, then press with the tines of a fork to create a ridged impression (these ridges will help the sauce to stick). Add the gnocchi to boiling salted water, after a few seconds they will swim up to the surface. Scoop them out before dressing immediately with your chosen sauce.

Green gnocchi are made by adding a little cooked, well-drained and very finely chopped spinach. Another type of gnocchi is what is known as *gnocchi alla romana*, and these are made with semolina or polenta. This is boiled in milk, mixed with egg and nutmeg then cut out and layered in a dish, before being baked with butter and Parmesan.

Gnocchi are very moreish. Light and fluffy, it won't matter how many you have in front of you – you will eat them all. The primary thing to remember is that the potato should be fresh, not cooked in advance, which can make the gnocchi rubbery and leaden. **SERVES 4**

potato dumplings with
GORGONZOLA SAUCE

Make the gnocchi as described opposite.

Meanwhile, make the sauce. Melt the butter in a pan and add the Gorgonzola or Dolcelatte. Break the cheese up with a fork and add enough cream to give the sauce the desired smooth, rich consistency.

Add the cooked gnocchi to the sauce, season with salt and pepper and sprinkle with Parmesan. Serve immediately.

1 recipe potato gnocchi (see left)
salt and pepper
60g Parmesan, freshly grated

Sauce
60g unsalted butter
50g Gorgonzola or Dolcelatte
    cheese, in chunks
a little double cream as required

In a way this simple, yet delicious dish can be seen to represent the colours of the Italian flag – green, red and white. **SERVES 4**

gnocchi with tomato
& MOZZARELLA

Make the gnocchi by mixing together the potatoes, flour, spinach and egg, adding more flour if the dough is too wet. Season lightly.

Make the simple tomato sauce by frying the garlic in the olive oil until soft, a few minutes. Add the tomatoes, basil, and some salt and pepper, and cook for 20 minutes.

Cook the gnocchi as per the recipe on page 76. When ready, drain, then add the sauce, Parmesan and some pepper, and mix well.

Divide the gnocchi between the plates, sprinkling over the mozzarella cubes and some more basil leaves to finish.

500g mashed floury potatoes
110g plain flour
200g spinach, cooked and
    squeezed dry (see page 18)
    and very finely chopped
1 egg
salt and pepper
40g Parmesan, freshly grated
150g buffalo mozzarella, cut into
    small cubes

Tomato sauce
1 garlic clove, peeled and
    finely chopped
6 tbsp olive oil
500g canned chopped tomatoes
6 basil leaves

POLENTA

Polenta is the name for a maize or corn flour, and for the dishes made from it. Maize reached Europe via Spain, imported from the Americas following the great discoveries of the sixteenth century. Easy to cultivate, and cropping well, it was immediately adopted by the Italians, especially in the north where the growing conditions were optimal.

After a long period out of fashion – it was seen as a food of poverty for many decades – polenta has made a comeback in home cooking as well as in good restaurants, where it is offered with all sorts of sauces. It used to be quite a job cooking polenta because it takes about 40 minutes of stirring. Now however, a pre-cooked 'quick' polenta has been developed, which takes only 5 minutes to cook. Although in my opinion this is not as tasty as the original, it is quite acceptable.

Polenta has various functions, mostly as an accompaniment to a sauce or stew, which could be of chicken, rabbit or sausages, or wild mushrooms (or a mixture). It can be eaten fresh, with the addition of grated Parmesan and butter, which changes the texture, making it ideal to accompany roasts instead of mashed potato. It can also be cooked fresh and then left to solidify, after which it can be cut in slices and fried or grilled to make the perfect accompaniment for any meat or vegetable.

A delightful and simple little dish from Venice, where the little pink shrimps of the lagoon taste very nice indeed. **SERVES 4**

quick polenta
WITH SHRIMPS

In a saucepan, bring the water to the boil with some salt and add the polenta slowly, stirring well, so that you don't produce lumps. After 5 minutes add the Parmesan and butter, and mix well.

In another pan, gently fry the shrimps in the butter for 5 minutes, before adding the lemon juice.

Pour the polenta on to individual serving plates, spooning the shrimp sauce over the top and serve.

1 litre water
salt
200g quick polenta
120g Parmesan, freshly grated
100g unsalted butter

Sauce
300g pink shrimps, shelled
50g unsalted butter
juice of 2 lemons

My granny used to make a large maize cake to be put in the oven when she was making bread. The resulting crunchy polenta pieces, which we ate with braised chicory, were stunning, and inspired this recipe. **SERVES 6**

polenta crust with
BRAISED CHICORY

Put the polenta in a bowl, add a pinch of salt and pepper and 2 tbsp olive oil and mix well. Pour in the boiling water and stir to make a dough. Divide the dough into 6 pieces and shape into hamburger-sized cakes.

Pour a little olive oil into a large frying pan and heat gently. Add the cakes and shallow-fry for 8 minutes on one side, until a thick crust has formed. Pour in a little more oil, turn the cakes over and repeat.

Meanwhile, put the olive oil, chilli, capers and garlic in a pan and cook gently, covered, for about 3 minutes. Add the chicory and water, and crumble in the stock cube. Reduce the heat and cook, covered, until the chicory has released a lot of its juices and is tender, about 15–20 minutes.

Arrange the polenta and the chicory on plates and spoon over a little of the chicory cooking juices to finish.

200g quick polenta
salt and pepper
olive oil
150ml boiling water

Braised chicory
6 tbsp olive oil
½ small fresh red chilli, chopped
1 tbsp salted capers, soaked (see page 24), drained and chopped
2 garlic cloves, peeled and chopped
600g Belgian chicory, roughly chopped
300ml water
1 chicken stock cube

This is a typical leftover dish, for when you have made too much polenta. Because cold polenta solidifies, you can cut it into crumbs, slices or shapes, which can be used for baked dishes like this, or fried or grilled. However, this dish can also be made with fresh polenta, which you leave to cool. **SERVES 6**

polenta bake with
CHEESE & TOMATOES

Preheat the oven to 225°C/Gas 7.

In an ovenproof dish, make a layer of some of the polenta chunks. Sprinkle some of the tomato sauce on top, with some of the Taleggio and a little Parmesan. Make more layers similarly, and finish with tomato sauce, the remaining Taleggio and a sprinkling of Parmesan.

Bake in the preheated oven for about 30 minutes, until a nice crust is visible and the cheese has melted. Cut the butter into small pieces and put on top. Serve immediately.

800g cooked and solidified
  polenta, in chunks
1 recipe tomato sauce
  (see page 55)
200g Taleggio cheese, in chunks
100g Parmesan, freshly grated
50g unsalted butter

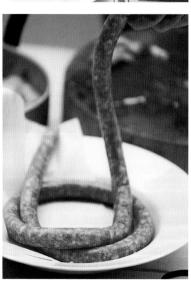

LEFTOVERS

Obviously, if you have any leftover polenta, it will set, and you can then use it in any number of ways – cut into slices then fried or grilled to accompany anything you like. One of my friends likes it at breakfast with bacon and tomatoes! In the Aosta Valley, they break it into pieces into hot milk, and eat it like porridge, often with sugar!

I have very fond memories of Nina Burgai of the Aosta Valley, who used to have a hotel above Champorcher that could only be reached by a funicular railway, as it was 2,000 metres high. Whenever you went there she would be making a rich yet delicious polenta – this is the recipe she taught me. **SERVES 4**

polenta with chicken
& SAUSAGE STEW

Bring the water to the boil with a little salt added. Pour the polenta in slowly and cook, stirring, until thickened and smooth, about 5–6 minutes. Add the Fontina cubes, butter and grated Parmesan and stir to combine.

In another pan, fry the onion in olive oil until soft, about 5 minutes, then add the chicken and sausage pieces. Allow to brown slightly, then add the wine and some salt and pepper. Cook for 5 minutes then add the tomatoes and cook until everything is tender, about 20 minutes.

Spoon the polenta and *ragù* on to the same plate, and enjoy!

1.5 litres water
salt and pepper
300g quick polenta
150g Fontina cheese, cut
   into cubes
150g unsalted butter
150g Parmesan, freshly grated

Chicken and sausage stew
1 large onion, peeled and
   finely chopped
8 tbsp olive oil
400g chicken meat, in chunks
200g *luganica* sausage, skinned,
   or home-made sausage in
   little chunks (see page 100)
100ml dry white wine
800g canned chopped tomatoes

RICE

Rice has only been established in Italy for 400 or 500 years. Introduced by the Arabs, it quickly became a welcome alternative to the wheat grain used for bread and pasta. Funnily enough, its cultivation started in the south of the country, where water was never going to be found in the quantities needed for the grain to grow happily. Since then production has moved to the northern regions of Piedmont, Lombardy and Veneto, where a supply of abundant water from the Alps has created the perfect conditions for growing the grain.

The Italians developed, from the original 'Japonica', the type of rice they wanted for risottos: a grain that was able to absorb enough water while cooking without falling apart, yet still remaining to the tooth (*al dente*). Various kinds of rice are produced in the Po Valley, from Vercelli in Piedmont to Venice in Veneto. The best rice for risotto are *arborio, vialone nano, Roma* and *carnaroli*. Anything else will not do!

This is a classic dish symbolising its region – in this case Lombardy, the region most associated with rice. Saffron is always included and sometimes bone marrow. If you omit the saffron, you will have the most basic of risottos.

SERVES 4

risotto
WITH SAFFRON

Bring the stock to the boil in a pan and keep it at a low simmer.

In a dry frying pan, toast the saffron strands for a few seconds, being careful not to burn them.

Melt 50g of the butter in a large saucepan over a low heat and fry the onion until soft, about 10 minutes. Add the wine and let it evaporate, about 2–3 minutes. Add the rice and stir to coat with the butter for a minute, then start to add the hot stock, ladle by ladle. Avoid drowning the rice in stock and wait until each ladleful is absorbed before you add the next. After 10 minutes' cooking and stirring, add the saffron and some salt and pepper. Continue to cook and add stock in the same way until the rice is *al dente*, another 8–10 minutes, then add the rest of the butter and half the grated Parmesan.

Stir well and serve, sprinkling the remaining Parmesan on top.

2.5 litres chicken or
  vegetable stock
2g saffron strands
100g unsalted butter
1 large onion, peeled and
  finely chopped
100ml dry white wine
500g *arborio* risotto rice
salt and pepper
60g Parmesan, freshly grated

Perhaps together with risotto with truffles, risotto with ceps is the best-known of Italian rice dishes. Italians eat this only in season when the *porcino* (*Boletus edulis* or cep) is around, but the following recipe I have devised will enable you to enjoy a mushroom risotto throughout the year. Should you manage to find some fresh porcini, however, I urge you to try them, as the taste is truly sensational! **SERVES 4**

risotto
WITH MUSHROOMS

Put the stock in a pan, bring to the boil and keep at a low simmer.

Heat the olive oil or butter in a large saucepan over a low heat, add the onion and fry until soft, about 10 minutes. Add the button mushrooms and the porcini and cook for 5 minutes, until soft and lightly browned.

Add the rice and stir for a minute or two, then add one or two ladles of boiling stock. Stir continuously over the heat, adding stock a ladleful at a time as each addition is absorbed. After 18–20 minutes, check for the required *al dente* texture – the rice should be tender, but with a firm bite in the centre, and the risotto should be moist.

Remove the pan from the heat, add the Parmesan and butter and stir in well. Season to taste and serve on warm plates. *Buon appetito.*

2 litres chicken or vegetable stock
4 tbsp olive oil or 50g
   unsalted butter
1 onion, peeled and very
   finely chopped
300g firm button mushrooms,
   finely sliced
50g dried porcini (ceps),
   rehydrated and chopped
350g *carnaroli* or *arborio*
   risotto rice
60g Parmesan, freshly grated
80g unsalted butter
salt and pepper

This is a Sicilian speciality, which is offered in bars and cafés as a small meal or snack. The rice is usually cooked specifically, and two versions are commonly offered, one filled with meat *ragù*, another with butter and mozzarella. They are the size of an orange, which is why they have the Italian name *arancini* (little oranges). The fashion has spread all over Italy and abroad as well. This version of mine can be made with leftover risotto, even a black risotto made with cuttlefish ink. Made in smaller sizes, as here, they are ideal for party finger food. **MAKES 24 RICE BALLS**

little
RICE BALLS

Put the leftover risotto in a bowl, and add half of the egg mixture, some salt, pepper, a pinch of nutmeg and Parmesan. Mix well with wet hands, then shape into apricot-sized balls.

Place the remaining beaten egg on one plate and the breadcrumbs on another. Roll the rice balls first in the egg, then in the breadcrumbs, then shallow- or deep-fry in hot oil on all sides until golden, about 5 minutes or so. Drain on kitchen paper, and serve warm or cold.

400g leftover risotto of any kind
4 eggs, beaten
salt and pepper
freshly grated nutmeg
50g Parmesan, freshly grated
100g dried white
    breadcrumbs
vegetable oil, for shallow- or
    deep-frying

The simplest and most sophisticated dish ever, which can be sublime with the fresh Alba truffle when in season, but can also be made with the much more economical black truffle, or even just with truffle butter and some summer truffle for decoration. **SERVES 4**

truffle
RISOTTO

Bring the stock to the boil in a pan and keep it at a low simmer.

In a large shallow pan, melt the truffle butter and fry the onion until soft, about 7 minutes. Add the wine and let it evaporate, then add the rice and stir for a minute. Add the hot stock, ladle by ladle, adding more as it is absorbed by the rice.

After 18–20 minutes, taste a grain to see if it is *al dente*. At this point, take the risotto off the heat and stir in the butter and Parmesan. Season to taste with salt and pepper.

Serve with the truffle thinly sliced on top of each portion.

80g truffle butter
2 litres good chicken, beef or
    vegetable stock
1 large onion, peeled and very
    finely chopped
50ml dry white wine
350g *carnaroli* or *arborio*
    risotto rice
30g unsalted butter
80g Parmesan, freshly grated
salt and pepper
1 x 60g black or white truffle

This risotto, with its base of poached, boned red mullet and lemon sole has a lovely, creamy texture. It is quite a work-intensive recipe but it is really worth it! I have chosen to use vialone nano rice for this dish. It is short-grained and very absorbent, which makes the risotto much tastier. **SERVES 4–6**

seafood
RISOTTO

Bring the water for the stock to the boil in a large pan with the onion, carrot, celery and parsley leaves and boil for 15 minutes. Add the red mullet and sole and poach gently for a further 10 minutes. Remove the fish from the stock and fillet, discarding the bones, heads and skin. Set the fish flesh aside. Remove the flavourings from the fish stock and keep at a simmer.

Fry the onion in another large pan in the olive oil until soft, about 5 minutes. Add the mussels and the wine, cover and steam for a few minutes until the mussels open. Remove the mussels from the pan, discarding any that remain closed. Working quickly, extract the mussel meat from the shells. Reserve the meat and a few shells for decoration, discarding the rest.

To the same pan add the scampi, octopus or squid, shrimps and the reserved fish flesh and mussel meat. Add the rice, stirring so that it is coated with the oil. Add the simmering stock, ladle by ladle, as it is absorbed by the rice. The rice should be cooked in 20–25 minutes.

Serve with a little extra virgin olive oil and a few drops of lemon juice.

1 large onion, peeled and
 finely sliced
6 tbsp olive oil
20 mussels, cleaned
150ml white wine
100g scampi or large
 prawns, shelled
100g baby octopus or squid
170g cooked shrimps, shelled
500g *vialone nano* risotto rice
extra virgin olive oil
juice of 1 lemon

Fish stock
1.5 litres water
1 small onion, peeled
1 carrot
a few celery and parsley leaves
2 red mullet, about 150g each
1 lemon sole, about 300g

meat

Needless to say, for this dish I would use one of those chickens which has lived in the courtyard and eaten the odd seed and piece of corn scratched out of the soil – naturally free-range. Italians like this simple dish, which is good hot or cold. **SERVES 4**

chicken baked with
ROSEMARY & GARLIC

Preheat the oven to 200°C/Gas 6. Put the chicken into a casserole or baking tray. Add the garlic and rosemary and then pour in the olive oil. Sprinkle with salt and pepper to taste, then mix with your hands to coat everything well with oil.

Put the chicken into the preheated oven and bake for 45 minutes. Pour in the wine and mix well.

Cook for a further 45 minutes, remove from the oven and serve with spinach or green salad.

1 x 2kg good chicken
8 garlic heads, whole
2 sprigs rosemary
6 tbsp olive oil
salt and pepper
150ml dry white wine

This sauce, known as *avgolemono*, comes originally from Greece, and was incorporated a long time ago into the southern Italian culinary repertoire. I usually make it to accompany lamb, but with a good free-range chicken, it will taste heavenly. **SERVES 4–6**

chicken with lemon
& EGG SAUCE

Dust all the pieces of chicken with flour seasoned with salt and pepper, shaking off the surplus.

Heat the olive oil in a pan until it nearly sizzles, add the onion and fry gently until soft, about 10 minutes. Add the chicken and, occasionally stirring, cook for 20 minutes until browned on all sides. Pour in the wine and cook gently for another 20 minutes. When the chicken is cooked, remove from the heat.

Meanwhile, mix together the eggs, lemon juice, garlic, plenty of freshly ground pepper and the parsley, seasoning to taste with salt.

Pour this mixture on to the chicken while still hot. Stir to coat all the pieces of chicken: the sauce should just thicken without becoming scrambled egg (rather similar to a spaghetti carbonara).

1.5kg chicken thighs or breasts, skin on, cut into plum-sized morsels
plain flour, to coat
salt and pepper
6 tbsp olive oil
1 onion, peeled and finely chopped
50ml dry white wine

Sauce
2 whole eggs and 2 egg yolks, beaten together
juice of 1 lemon
1 garlic clove, peeled and puréed
1 tbsp finely chopped parsley

We used to eat this in our house when money was short but we still wanted the taste of meat. My mother had a magical ability to transform minced beef into a succulent meatloaf, which was sliced to accompany a pasta, flavoured with the produced sauce. A complete meal in one! **SERVES 6**

meatloaf in
TOMATO SAUCE

Preheat the oven to 180°C/Gas 4.

Put both minces in a large bowl and add the eggs, cheese, breadcrumbs, garlic, salt and pepper. Mix very well together, then shape with your hands into a nice oval shape, rather like a loaf of bread.

In a large 3 litre casserole, which should be big enough to hold the loaf and its sauce, heat the olive oil and gently fry the loaf until brown all over. Turn it gently so as not to break it. Now add the onions and fry until soft, about 10 minutes. Add the tomatoes and basil to the casserole until the loaf is covered (add water if necessary). Cover with the lid or some foil.

Now let it cook in the preheated oven for 2 hours. Check from time to time: if it looks as if it needs additional moisture, add a little water. Taste for salt and pepper.

Let the meatloaf rest for 10 minutes. (If you wish to serve the meatloaf with pasta you should cook it in plenty of boiling salted water for about 8–10 minutes during this time). Lift the meatloaf – carefully! – from the sauce, cut into slices and serve with the sauce and pasta, if desired.

750g lean minced beef
750g lean minced pork
6 eggs, beaten
100g Parmesan, freshly grated
150g fresh white breadcrumbs
2 garlic cloves, peeled and
   finely puréed
salt and pepper
8 tbsp olive oil
2 large onions, peeled and
   finely chopped
800g canned chopped tomatoes
10 basil leaves
500g *rigatoni* or *penne* (optional)

This dish is truly wonderful when using the fresh sausages made by the local Norcian master butchers, who are known as *norcini*. As they may be difficult to find, I suggest making the sausages from scratch instead – it's not too complicated, and it is well worth it. You can get hold of Castelluccio lentils, the Italian Puy lentils, in a good delicatessen. **SERVES 4**

lentil & home-made
SAUSAGE STEW

For the lentils, fry the garlic and the sun-dried tomatoes in 6 tbsp of the olive oil for a few minutes in a large pan. When the garlic starts to turn pale golden, add the lentils, stock and celery, and cook for 30 minutes or until the lentils are soft. Cover and keep warm over a low heat.

Meanwhile, in a medium-sized bowl, mix the sausage ingredients together well and season with salt and pepper. Take a handful of mince and roll it into a sausage shape, 8cm long and 3cm in diameter. Wrap tightly in a piece of foil, closing by turning the ends as you would a sweet.

Bring a large pan of water to the boil. Poach the sausages in the boiling water until they pop up to the surface, about 2–3 minutes. Leave to cool a little, then take off the foil. This poaching should ensure that the sausages hold together.

Moisten the sausages with the remaining olive oil, then fry or grill (or roast) until golden on all sides, about 5 minutes.

Add the sausages to the warm lentils, and allow to cook gently together for 5 minutes. Eat with bread or, if you like, with a few boiled potatoes.

2 garlic cloves, peeled and
   squashed
50g sun-dried tomatoes, cut
   into strips
7 tbsp extra virgin olive oil
250g Castelluccio lentils
450ml chicken stock
2 celery stalks, with leaves,
   chopped
salt and pepper

Sausages
500g minced pork
50ml strong red wine
1 tsp fennel seeds
1 mild chilli, finely chopped
1 tsp chopped rosemary
salt and pepper

Meat cooked the Milanese way is almost always breaded and fried. The most typical example is usually made with veal, but the dish is also possible with chicken or pork. For this one here, you need a large pork cutlet with the bone, the flesh beaten quite thinly. The rest is child's play. **SERVES 4**

milanese breaded pork
CUTLET WITH BROCCOLI

Place the cutlets on a piece of clingfilm or greaseproof paper, and cover with another piece. Beat the fleshy parts with a mallet or something heavy. You want the meat to spread and become a little thinner. Remove the film or paper.

Dip the cutlets in the beaten eggs, then coat with breadcrumbs.

Pour enough mixed oil into a large shallow pan to cover the base. Heat it until it starts to bubble, then fry the cutlets on a medium-high heat for at least 5 minutes on each side until golden brown. Set aside and keep warm.

Blanch the sprouting broccoli in a large saucepan of boiling water for a few minutes before gently frying in a pan with the sliced garlic, chopped chilli and a little olive oil until softened. Serve with the cutlets and the lemon quarters.

4 large pork cutlets, bone in
2 eggs, beaten with some salt
   and pepper
about 6 tbsp dried white
   breadcrumbs
plenty of olive oil and vegetable
   oil, for shallow-frying
500g purple sprouting broccoli
2 garlic cloves, peeled and sliced
½ chilli, chopped
1 lemon, quartered

This dish reminds me of Tuscany where the good local meat of the Val di Chiana, a valley near Florence, makes very worthwhile eating. It is important here that you do not overcook the meat, as you want it to retain all of its natural succulence. **SERVES 4**

sliced
BEEF

Pour enough olive oil into your frying pan to cover the base generously, and heat gently. Salt the steaks, add to the pan and shallow-fry for 5 minutes on each side, until browned but still rare.

In a separate small pan, warm up the extra virgin olive oil, peppercorns and rosemary over a low heat.

To serve, cut the steaks into 2cm strips. Arrange the steak slices onto four plates and drizzle over the peppery rosemary oil. *Buon appetito.*

8 tbsp olive oil, for shallow-frying
4 topside steaks, about 200g each
salt

Sauce
12 tbsp extra virgin olive oil
2 tbsp green peppercorns
4 sprigs rosemary, divided into
    smaller sprigs

This classic Sunday dish of the Neapolitans is a *piatto unico* – an all-in-one dish that is served as a main course. The *braciola* is a sort of beef olive with a special filling, reminiscent of Arab cooking. These are relatively complicated to produce, but on Sundays everybody has time to prepare something so delicious. Neapolitans make home-made *fusilli* to accompany their beef olives, and I think my old nanny Lina used to make the best. **SERVES 4–6**

neapolitan
BEEF OLIVE STEW

To make the beef olives, line up the escalopes side by side on your work surface. Make a stuffing mixture by combining the breadcrumbs, drained raisins, pine kernels, garlic, half the Parmesan and parsley, and seasoning to taste. Divide the mixture evenly between the centres of the escalopes. Roll up each of the escalopes to enclose the stuffing and secure with a couple of wooden toothpicks.

Meanwhile, start to prepare the sauce by frying the onions in the olive oil in a large pan. When the onions are soft, after about 6–7 minutes, add the beef olives, and brown on each side. Add the wine and boil to allow the alcohol to evaporate. Add the tomato *passata* and the diluted tomato pureé and bring to the boil.

Reduce the heat, cover and let it bubble gently for 2 hours, turning the beef olives occasionally. When ready, add salt and pepper to taste and stir in the basil. Keep the beef olives separate from the sauce.

6 beef escalopes, quite thinly cut
3 tbsp fresh white breadcrumbs
40g raisins, soaked in water
   and drained
80g pine kernels
1 garlic clove, peeled and puréed
100g Parmesan, freshly grated
4 tbsp coarsely chopped
   flat-leaf parsley
salt and pepper

Sauce
2 large onions, peeled and sliced
about 6 tbsp olive oil
100ml dry white wine
800g tomato *passata* or tomato
   pulp (*polpa di pomodoro*)
2 tbsp tomato pureé, diluted
   with 2 tbsp water
a few basil leaves, shredded

To make the pasta, pile the flour into a mound on a work surface and make a well in the middle. Add the egg and a splash of water. Gradually mix into the flour, adding enough water to bind the dough. Knead until smooth, then cover with a cloth and leave to rest for about 30 minutes.

Dust your work surface with a little flour and shape the dough a little at a time. Take a little piece of dough and roll it under the palm of your hand to make a baton, about 10cm long and 3mm in diameter. With a thin skewer, press the little baton around the skewer to make a spiral shape. Let the pasta spiral run down and off the skewer, then put on a cloth. Repeat to shape the rest of the dough.

Cook the pasta in plenty of boiling salted water until *al dente*, about 3–4 minutes. Drain and dress with the sauce.

Cut the beef olives into slices and arrange on top of the pasta. Scatter the remaining Parmesan over the pasta to serve.

Pasta
500g durum wheat flour, plus
   extra to dust
1 egg, beaten

For this recipe the lamb cutlets have to be larger than usual, so that they can be stuffed. Get the butcher to cut eight cutlets on the bone, of 2.5–3cm thickness (which means a double cutlet, with the meat of two bones, one of the bones removed). These lamb cutlets are wonderful hot, but are also great cold as part of a picnic. **SERVES 4**

stuffed
LAMB CUTLETS

With a sharp pointed knife, make an incision in the flesh of each cutlet, from the side opposite the bone, to make a pocket. Stuff the pockets with the ham, sage and cheese. Press the sides together to seal the cutlets. Dip the cutlets in the beaten eggs first, then coat well with dried breadcrumbs.

Pour enough olive oil into a large frying pan to cover the base generously and heat gently. Fry the cutlets until brown, about 5–6 minutes per side if you like them juicy as I do. Drain on kitchen paper and serve. Courgettes with Green Beans and Mint (see page 14) makes a delicious accompaniment.

8 large (double) young lamb cutlets, French trimmed, fat removed
2 slices Parma ham or *speck*, quartered
8 sage leaves
8 small pieces Fontina cheese, sliced
2 eggs, beaten with salt and pepper
about 6 tbsp dried white breadcrumbs
olive oil, for shallow-frying

This dish is often found in Venice, where it is called *fegato all veneziano*. It can also be made with pork, lamb or chicken livers. Whichever you use, the result is always satisfying, and is particularly tasty when served with a purée of potatoes and celeriac. **SERVES 4**

calf's liver
WITH ONIONS

Dust the liver slices with flour.

Heat the olive oil in a large frying pan over a low heat, add the onion and cook gently until soft, about 10–15 minutes.

Add the raisins, sugar and the flour-dusted liver and shallow-fry gently for 7 minutes, until cooked to your liking.

Pour in the vinegar and season with salt and pepper to taste, then stir to heat through. Serve immediately.

600g calf's liver, trimmed and finely sliced
plain flour, to dust
8 tbsp olive oil
600g white onions, peeled and very thinly sliced
50g raisins
20g caster sugar
4 tbsp white wine vinegar
salt and pepper

PARMA HAM FAT

Parma ham fat may be difficult to find in this proportion outside of Italy (but get to know your local deli well!). Instead you could use *lardo*, the Italian lard, which is preserved in pieces and rolled as you would bacon. The rendered pork lard is not the same thing at all, but you could use it as a last resort: it is already a paste, which you can mix with the herbs.

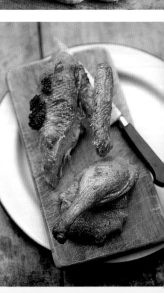

Where else would a dish like this be cooked if not in the 'fatherland' of poetry and pigs? Emilia Romagna, of course. The ducks of the area are the proper ones with large breasts and some natural fat, which are fed mainly on corn. The pigs are the famous animals which produce that wonderful fatty ham known here as Parma ham. This dish represents a perfect harmony between the two. **SERVES 4–6**

roast duck with
PARMA HAM FAT

Preheat the oven to 200°C/Gas 6.

Mix the ham fat or lard with the peppercorns, garlic, a pinch of nutmeg, cinnamon, rosemary and sage until you have a solid paste.

In a roasting tin, coat the duck with the olive oil, and sprinkle a little salt inside and outside. Spread the fatty paste on to the duck breasts, then cover the roasting tin with foil. Roast the duck in the preheated oven for an hour. Remove the foil and return to the oven for a further 30 minutes, basting with the copious fat.

Serve the duck meat with pieces of the delicious skin.

200g Parma ham fat (from a
    friendly grocer), finely minced
    or chopped, or pork lard
10g black peppercorns, crushed
1 garlic clove, peeled and puréed
freshly grated nutmeg
a pinch of ground cinnamon
1 tbsp each of rosemary needles
    and sage leaves, finely chopped
1 x 2kg free-range duck
4 tbsp olive oil
salt

fish

This cooking method, designed to keep in all the juices and aromas, has been in use since Roman times. Then, they would cook foods enclosed in terracotta, while now we wrap in foil and oven-bake to achieve the same result. So long as the little packages are well sealed, you could also try cooking this on a charcoal grill. **SERVES 4**

trout
BAKED IN FOIL

Preheat the oven to 200°C/Gas 6. Have ready 4 pieces of foil large enough to wrap the fish fairly loosely.

Clean the trout and remove the scales and all the innards (or get your fishmonger to do this). Wash the trout, and dry them. Cut off the fins. Make 4 incisions in one side of each fish with a knife.

Arrange the 4 pieces of foil on your work surface, and on each, place 4 slices of lemon. In the cavity of each fish, put some salt and pepper, a quarter of the herbs and 15g butter, cut into small pieces. Close the trout and place each one on top of the lemon slices on the foil, cut-side up. Divide the remaining butter, in pieces, between the fish, rubbing into the cuts. Season each fish with salt and pepper, then add another 4 lemon slices to the top of each. Close the foil around each fish to produce a bag.

Bake in the preheated oven for just 20 minutes. The fish are delicious served with a simple boiled potato salad.

4 rainbow trout, about 250g each
32 thin slices of lemon
salt and pepper
1 little bunch chervil, divided
  into 4
1 bunch parsley, divided into 4
100g unsalted butter

In Napoli they use both salted and fresh cod. Because it is easier to come by, and does not involve the lengthy process of washing and de-salting associated with the salted variety, I have suggested you use fresh cod here (though you can substitute it for the salted cod should you wish). This dish is excellent served just with some freshly boiled waxy potatoes. **SERVES 4**

cod with tomatoes
& OLIVES

Pour 2 tbsp of the olive oil into a large frying pan and heat gently. Coat the steaks with the flour, add to the pan and fry for 5 minutes on each side. Drain on kitchen paper and set aside.

In another pan, put the remaining 6 tbsp olive oil and fry the garlic slices for a few minutes, until just before they change colour. Add the tomatoes, olives, oregano, salt and pepper, and fry for 5 minutes.

Put the steak in the pan with the rest of the ingredients and heat minimally to absorb the flavours. Serve with boiled potatoes.

4 fresh cod steaks, about
   150g each
plain flour, to coat
8 tbsp olive oil
2 garlic cloves, peeled and sliced
400g canned chopped tomatoes
60g pitted black olives
1 tbsp fresh oregano or
   1 tsp dried
salt and pepper

Muddica is a sort of magic ingredient for Sicilians. Basically, it is fresh, flavoured breadcrumbs, which are used in a variety of ways – to stuff sardines, to coat a slice of fish to be grilled, as here, or even as a cheap, delicious alternative to sprinkling Parmesan on pasta. **SERVES 4**

grilled breaded
SWORDFISH

Preheat the grill to medium-hot, and have the fish steaks at room temperature.

Place the breadcrumbs, olive oil, garlic and parsley in a bowl and season to taste with salt and pepper. Mix the ingredients with your fingers to obtain almost moist but loose breadcrumbs. Coat the fish steaks with the breadcrumb mixture on both sides.

Put the coated steaks under the preheated grill and cook for 5 minutes on each side. Serve with a rocket and chicory salad.

4 swordfish (or tuna) steaks,
   about 150g each
150g fresh white breadcrumbs,
   finely processed
2 tbsp extra virgin olive oil
1 garlic clove, peeled and puréed
1 tbsp very finely chopped
   parsley
salt and pepper

In a few restaurants offering southern Italian food, you may find this curious recipe. I have called it *alla aqua pazza*, which translates literally as cooked in 'mad water', though it is often found as *all'acqua di mare*, as it is usually cooked in sea water. As sea water may be difficult to come by, here I have simply added salt to ordinary water to re-create the effect. **SERVES 4**

poached
SEA BREAM

Put the fish in a shallow pan large enough to take both with not much space around them. Divide the herbs and lemon slices between the fish, pushing them into the cavities. Pour in the water and oil, which should cover the fish. Add the salt and peppercorns.

Put the pan on the stove and bring to the boil quickly. Reduce the heat and simmer slowly for 15–18 minutes. Serve the fish with boiled Savoy cabbage.

2 x 600g sea bream, cleaned
1 bunch flat-leaf parsley
1 bunch chervil
16 lemon slices
500ml water
200ml olive oil
50g salt
a few black peppercorns

These little fish, which, like mackerel, contain oils that are beneficial to our health, are popular throughout the Mediterranean. This quick, tasty dish can also be eaten in smaller portions as a wonderful *antipasto*. **SERVES 4**

grilled fresh sardines
WITH GREEN SALSA

Preheat the barbecue or charcoal grill to hot.

Mix the *salmoriglio* ingredients together in a small bowl.

Put the sardines directly onto a hot charcoal grill. Sprinkle them with salt, brush with a little of the *salmoriglio* and cook for 5 minutes per side. Serve the sardines either hot or cold, with the lemon quarters and the remainder of the *salmoriglio*.

16 large fresh sardines, gutted
    and cleaned
salt and pepper
1 lemon, cut into quarters

Salmoriglio
150ml extra virgin olive oil
juice of 2 lemons, finely grated
    rind of 1
1 small chilli, finely chopped
1 garlic clove, peeled and very
    finely chopped
4 tbsp finely chopped parsley

A flavoursome fish packed with healthy oils, Mackerel is not appreciated as much as it ought to be – while many people love it, others are indifferent, but cooked and marinated this way, the fish assumes another dimension, which should please everybody. **SERVES 4**

marinated
FRIED MACKEREL

Dip the mackerel fillets in seasoned flour, and shake off the surplus. Pour enough olive oil into a large frying pan to cover the base generously and heat until it sizzles. Fry the fish fillets until golden on each side, about 5–7 minutes, depending on size. Set aside to cool.

Prepare the marinade by frying the onions in the olive oil until soft, about 5–7 minutes. Add the sugar, vinegar and mint leaves and season well with salt and pepper.

Make layers of fish fillets in a ceramic container, interspersing them with onion and herbs. Pour the remaining juice over the top and place in the fridge.

Serve the next day with some hot boiled potatoes. Alternatively, cut the fillets into slivers and add to a simple green salad.

4 large fresh mackerel, filleted
(get your fishmonger to do this)
plain flour, to dust
salt and pepper
olive oil, for shallow-frying

Marinade
2 large onions, finely sliced
100ml olive oil
30g caster sugar
100ml white wine vinegar
1 bunch mint

This interesting dish of small prawns is named after a man I met in Palermo while I was filming a series for BBC TV, who produced it for me on the roadside charcoal grill he was tending. To make it, you will need a rectangular aluminium tray, plus aluminium foil to cover. **SERVES 4**

michele's
PINK SHRIMPS

Put the shrimps in an aluminium tray, add the lemon juice, olive oil, garlic, parsley and some salt and pepper. Give it a mix, then add the brandy. Seal the tray with aluminium foil and place on a hot (preferably charcoal) grill. Leave to cook for 20 minutes.

These shrimps are wonderful eaten with your fingers!

500g very fresh pink shrimps
juice of 2 lemons (Sicilian if
    possible)
80ml olive oil
2 garlic cloves, peeled
    and halved
a handful of flat-leaf
    parsley leaves
salt and pepper
50ml brandy

Extremely simple but very impressive, this dish follows my cooking motto, MOF, MOF (Minimum Of Fuss, Maximum Of Flavour). However, you do need the freshest prawns you can lay your hands on. The wonderful Imperial prawns are best for this recipe, so talk to your fishmonger and see whether he can get hold of some for you. **SERVES 4**

giant prawns with
GARLIC, OIL & CHILLI

Peel only the body of the prawns, leaving the heads intact (they are full of juice).

Heat the olive oil in a large frying pan until it just starts to sizzle. Add the prawns and, over a high heat now, cook them on both sides until they change colour, head included. This should take about 3 minutes. Sprinkle with lemon juice, and add the garlic and chilli.

Serve the prawns on a portion of the sauce in individual bowls. To eat, remove the heads from the prawns and squeeze all the wonderful juices into the sauce.

16 fresh giant prawns
100ml olive oil
juice of 1 lemon
3 garlic cloves, peeled and sliced
1 red chilli, finely chopped

Impepata is a southern Italian dialect word for a dish full of pepper, usuallly applied to a dish of black mussels, with a few other shellfish when available. I have suggested clams here, but some razor clams, if small enough, would be a delightful addition. **SERVES 4–6**

shellfish
FRICASSEE

Heat the olive oil in a large saucepan and fry the garlic and chilli for 1–2 minutes. Add all the shellfish, along with the wine and parsley. Put the lid on and cook until all the shells are open, about 4 minutes, shaking the pan occasionally. They should start to open quite quickly, but keep on the heat until all the shells are open. Discard any shells that remain closed.

Add lots of black pepper. Stir well and serve in bowls, with lots of bread to mop up the sauce.

100ml extra virgin olive oil
2 garlic cloves, peeled and
    coarsely chopped
1 small fresh red chilli,
    finely chopped
1.5kg black mussels, cleaned
    and prepared
1.5kg large clams, cleaned
    and prepared
500ml dry white wine
3 tbsp finely chopped
    flat-leaf parsley
abundant freshly and coarsely
    ground black pepper

What could be more wonderful in the height of summer than a lovely, freshly made seafood salad, eaten with *grissini* and washed down with a glass or two of crisp, dry, chilled white wine! The combination of fish to choose from is endless. Here are some suggestions: small razor clams, clams, prawns, small octopus, squid, cuttlefish, black mussels, scallops, etc. The choice is yours.

SERVES 4

seafood
SALAD

Cook the seafood for a few minutes in a saucepan of boiling salted water. Drain well and put in a large bowl.

Mix together the olive oil, lemon juice, garlic, finely chopped parsley and lots of pepper, and dress the seafood. This salad can be eaten either hot or cold.

600g freshly prepared and raw
   seafood (see above)
salt and pepper
50ml extra virgin olive oil
juice of 1 lemon
2 garlic cloves, peeled
   and halved
2 tbsp finely chopped
   flat-leaf parsley

vegetables

Very fashionable, grilled vegetables are available in almost every restaurant, whether Italian or not. At home you could either charcoal-grill these on a barbecue or use a special cast-iron ridged grill pan. The most important thing to remember is to add flavour with a marinade into which you dip the vegetables and which you use for basting as well. **SERVES 4**

grilled
VEGETABLES

Preheat a charcoal grill or ridged grill pan.

Prepare the marinade by mixing together all the ingredients. Dip the vegetables one by one into the marinade, place on the hot grill and cook for a few minutes each side. You will have to do this in batches. Leave the cooking of the tomatoes until last as they will make the grill wet. When turning the vegetables on to the other side, baste with the rest of the marinade.

Eat either as accompaniment to main dishes, or as a first course.

1 aubergine, thinly sliced
   lengthways
2 courgettes, thinly sliced
   lengthways
1 red pepper, seeded and cut
   into strips
1 yellow pepper, seeded and cut
   into strips
4 tomatoes, halved

Marinade
5 tbsp extra virgin olive oil
2 tbsp very finely chopped mint
2 tbsp very finely chopped basil
2 tbsp white wine vinegar
salt and pepper

Here I have purposely chosen two ingredients which hail from the two furthest apart regions of Italy, Sicily and the Veneto. *Maccu* (a Sicilian dialect word) is a purée of dried skinned broad beans, which is often eaten by itself or with some braised bitter vegetables like chicory or rape tops. Radicchio, grown in the Veneto, is a slightly bitter type of chicory, which compliments the *maccu* well. **SERVES 4**

broad bean purée with
GRILLED RADICCHIO

Drain the broad beans, cover them with fresh water and cook slowly until dissolved into a purée, stirring from time to time, about 20 minutes. Heat 100ml of the olive oil with the garlic in a large pan until gently bubbling, not boiling. Put in the radicchio and capers and add the water. Put the lid on and braise until the radicchio is soft. After 15 minutes, take a sharp knife and pierce the base of the radicchio. If it goes in easily, the radicchio is ready.

Should the broad bean purée still not be very fine, put it through a food processor. Add 6 tbsp of extra virgin olive oil, and some salt and pepper. Serve the two on a plate next to one another and drizzle a little more extra virgin olive oil on top.

300g dried skinned broad beans, soaked overnight
extra virgin olive oil
1 garlic clove, peeled and sliced
4 heads radicchio or Belgian chicory, quartered
15g salted capers, soaked (see page 24)
50ml water
6 tbsp extra virgin olive oil
salt and pepper

Versatile, delicious and easy to make, *caponata* is probably Sicily's best-known dish. Throughout the centuries Sicily has been invaded and colonised by many other nations and many Sicilian recipes show influences from other cuisines. Here you will see that there are some hints of the French *ratatouille*, while the inclusion of raisins and pine kernels suggests some Arabic influences too.

SERVES 4–6

sicilian
VEGETABLE STEW

Cut the aubergine into 3cm chunks, soak in cold water for 5 minutes, then drain. This will stop the aubergine from absorbing too much oil.

Fry the onion in the olive oil in a large saucepan for a few minutes to soften. Put the aubergine chunks into the pan and fry until soft and tender, about 10 minutes. Add the tomatoes, diluted tomato purée, sugar, capers, olives, vinegar, celery leaves and stalks, raisins and some salt and pepper and stew slowly until everything is melted together, about 30 minutes.

Stir in the pine kernels, if desired, and serve either cold or warm as a side dish, or by itself with bread.

800g aubergine
1 large onion, peeled
  and chopped
2 tbsp olive oil
3 ripe tomatoes, cut into
  chunky cubes
1 tbsp tomato purée, diluted
  with a little water
1 tbsp caster sugar
1 tbsp salted capers, soaked
  (see page 24)
20 green pitted olives
1 tbsp white wine vinegar
chopped leaves and stalks
  of 1 head celery
1 tbsp raisins
salt and pepper
1 tbsp pine kernels (optional)

Vegetables, either simply steamed or boiled and dressed just with extra virgin olive oil and lemon juice, are to die for. Try if you can to get hold of Sicilian lemons or those from the Amalfi coast – their perfume and taste are unbeatable. **SERVES 4**

salad of
COOKED VEGETABLES

Put the carrots and fennel into a large pan of boiling salted water, and cook for 15 minutes. Then add the peppers, asparagus, beans and courgettes and cook for another 10 minutes, until soft. Remove from the heat, drain and leave to cool.

Once cooled, arrange the vegetables on a serving platter, making a display with a nice sense of colour and shape. Drizzle with the extra virgin olive oil and some drops of lemon juice. Season with a little salt and plenty of pepper and serve.

2 large carrots, peeled and cut into quarters
2 fennel bulbs, trimmed and sliced
salt and pepper
200g red peppers, seeded and cut into eighths
8 asparagus stalks, trimmed
100g French beans
2 courgettes, trimmed and cut into thick strips lengthways
good extra virgin olive oil
juice of 1 large fresh lemon

For this recipe the ingredients should be the freshest and best you can possibly buy. Baby artichokes should be tangerine-sized, with very little of the fluffly choke in their centres. This recipe is based loosely on the well-known artichokes *alla Judia*, so called because Jewish families introduced the dish to the Romans some 400 years ago. **SERVES 4**

braised
BABY ARTICHOKES

Trim the top 2cm of the artichokes, pull away the tough outer leaves and cut the bottom 4cm off the stem. With a sharp knife, trim the tougher tops of the leaves, leaving only the tender parts of the artichokes. Make an aperture in the centre of each artichoke and excavate the choke if it has already grown; if the artichoke is very young, this may not be necessary.

Pack the cleaned baby artichokes tightly next to one another in a suitable saucepan. Add the onion, capers and parsley. Pour in enough olive oil to reach halfway up the artichokes, then add enough water to raise the level of the swimming oil higher, almost to touch the top of the artichokes.

Cover with the lid and cook on a low heat for 30 minutes. The oil should just gently bubble. Try to pierce an artichoke with the tip of a sharp knife; if it penetrates easily, the artichoke will be cooked.

These artichokes are wonderful by themselves, hot, as a cold *antipasto*, or as a side dish.

12 baby artichokes
1 large onion, peeled and
  finely chopped
1 tbsp small salted capers, soaked
  (see page 24)
2 tbsp chopped flat-leaf parsley
lots of olive oil

This is not dissimilar to the French *quiche* which, although most known for its Lorraine connections, is actually made all over France. In Liguria, a similar egg tart is made, the *torta pasqualina* (Easter tart), of which this vegetarian tart is a variant. It is delicious eaten either hot or cold. **SERVES 6**

spinach &
ARTICHOKE TART

Preheat the oven to 180°C/Gas 4. Use a little olive oil to grease a 25cm tart tin, then dust with a little flour.

Blanch the spinach in boiling salted water for about 3 minutes, then drain well. Using your hands, squeeze the spinach leaves to extract as much liquid as possible. Chop finely.

Heat the olive oil and fry the onions briefly in a large saucepan. Add the water and the baby artichokes hearts, cover and cook until tender, about 20 minutes.

In a bowl, put the spinach, ricotta, beaten eggs, 50g of the Parmesan, a little nutmeg and some salt and pepper to taste. Mix together well.

Roll the pastry out until thin and use it to line the prepared tart tin. Pour the filling into the tin, sprinkle with the remaining grated Parmesan and bake in the preheated oven for 30 minutes. Leave to cool a little and then serve.

675g frozen shortcrust pastry
 (to cut corners)
olive oil
flour, to dust

Filling
1kg spinach leaves, cleaned,
 washed and any tough
 stalks removed
salt and pepper
6 tbsp olive oil
2 onions, peeled and thinly sliced
100ml water
6 baby artichoke hearts, trimmed
 (see page 135) and sliced
300g fresh ricotta cheese
6 eggs, beaten
70g Parmesan, freshly grated
freshly grated nutmeg

This recipe is self-explanatory, extremely simple to make and delicious. It makes a wonderful side dish for almost anything, and is particularly good with roast meat or poached fish. **SERVES 6–8**

baked potatoes with
ONION & GARLIC

Preheat the oven to 220°C/Gas 7.

Put the potatoes, onion and garlic in a baking tray, sprinkle with the olive oil, some salt and plenty of pepper and mix with your hands. Add the rosemary.

Bake in the preheated oven for 40–50 minutes. Halfway through, give everything a mix to allow the bottom layer to come to the top and become brown.

The garlic in the skin, squeezed with your fingers into your mouth, is creamy and sweet.

1.5kg potatoes, peeled and cut into thick slices
500g onions, peeled and sliced
30 garlic cloves, unpeeled
100ml olive oil
salt and pepper
1 sprig rosemary

I love fennel, either raw or cooked, and sometimes I eat it as a digestive. When buying your fennel, be sure to check the outer layer – it should be shiny, fresh and not too tough. This dish can be eaten either with bread or on its own as a starter, or served as an accompaniment to a main course – fish or meat.

SERVES 4

fennel
GRATIN

Preheat the oven to 200°C/Gas 6.

Cook the whole fennel bulbs in salted water until the point of a sharp knife enters easily, about 20–25 minutes. Drain and leave to cool.

Cut the fennel into 5mm slices and arrange them like roof tiles on a baking tray. Sprinkle with the cubed butter and the breadcrumbs, plus a little nutmeg, salt and pepper and bake in the preheated oven until the crust is golden, about another 20 minutes. Serve hot.

4 large fennel bulbs
salt and pepper
80g unsalted butter, cut
 into cubes
100g fresh white breadcrumbs
freshly grated nutmeg

This is a variation on the well known *parmigiana melanzane*, the baked dish of aubergines with tomato and mozzarella. By using Taleggio instead of mozzarella and courgette in place of aubergine, I've made this dish a little lighter, but no less wonderful! **SERVES 6–8**

baked courgettes with
TOMATO & TALEGGIO

Preheat the oven to 200°C/Gas 6.

Make the tomato sauce by frying the garlic in the olive oil in a pan until soft, about 5 minutes. Add the tomatoes and basil, some salt and pepper to taste and cook gently for 20–30 minutes.

To make the batter, put the flour in a bowl, make a well in the centre and pour in the beaten eggs. Season with a little nutmeg and some salt and pepper, and mix well to a thickish batter.

In a frying pan, gently heat a little olive oil. Dip the courgette slices into the batter, and fry in batches in the hot oil until golden, about 3–4 minutes per side. Drain on kitchen paper and set aside.

Now to assemble the dish. Put a layer of courgette slices on the base of a baking dish. Pour over a little tomato sauce, and some of the cheeses and then get on with the next layer. Finish with the tomato sauce and grated Parmesan.

Bake for 30 minutes in the preheated oven. Leave to cool before cutting into portions to serve.

olive oil, for shallow-frying
700g middle-sized courgettes, cut into 5mm thick slices lengthways
400g Taleggio cheese, cubed
100g Parmesan, freshly grated
salt and pepper

Tomato sauce
2 garlic cloves, peeled and finely sliced
6 tbsp olive oil
800g canned chopped tomatoes
10 basil leaves

Batter
100g plain flour
4 eggs, beaten
freshly grated nutmeg

desserts

An autumnal recipe using ripe pears and an uncomplicated red wine. This simple dish is very Italian, and has loads of flavour. **SERVES 6**

williams pears in
RED WINE SAUCE

Preheat the oven to 200°C/Gas 6.

Wash and put the pears upright in a suitably sized ovenproof container. You want them to fit snugly, without too much space between them. Bake in the preheated oven for 30–40 minutes.

Remove the pears from the oven and pour over the wine. Sprinkle over the lemon rind and most of the sugar, reserving a small amount to spoon on top of the pears. Bake for another 20 minutes, by which time the wine will have reduced and thickened in consistency.

Put the pears in a glass bowl, cover with the red wine syrup and chill.

Divide between 6 plates and serve with the syrup and some whipped double cream, if desired.

6 ripe Williams pears
400ml red wine
rind of 1 lemon, in pieces
150g caster sugar
whipped double cream
    (optional), to serve

An extremely simple recipe with lots of fresh flavour. The best mango to use here would be the Alfonso variety from India, but this recipe will be a success whatever type you use. **SERVES 4**

mango with
LIME SYRUP

To peel the mangoes, cut close to the large narrow stone along the length of the fruit on either side. You will have two rounded bits, and the stone. Cut the peel off the rounded bits and place the four pieces on a large plate.

To prepare the syrup, first cut the rind off the limes, leaving behind any pith. Slice this rind into thin strips. Squeeze the juice from the limes into a small pan and add the sugar. Simmer until the sugar has melted, then boil to reduce this liquid by half. Add the strips of rind and continue to simmer for a few minutes, until caramelised. Leave the syrup to cool.

Pour the cooled lime syrup over the mango halves and decorate with the mint sprigs.

2 large ripe mangoes
4 small sprigs mint

Lime syrup
3 limes
100g caster sugar

This terrific dessert is easy to make, delicious warm or cold and can be used in many different ways. It can be either eaten as it is, accompanied by some polenta biscuits (see page 153), used as a filling for choux pastry buns, or made into a wonderful ice cream. **SERVES 6**

zabaglione with bitter
CHOCOLATE SAUCE

Put the egg yolks and sugar in a heatproof bowl (preferably a copper pan with a rounded base) and whisk for a few minutes to obtain a smooth and pure foam. Add the chosen dessert wine and mix well.

Have ready a pan of boiling water, in which the bowl will fit, without the base touching the water. Put the bowl in place in the pan, and beat continuously over the simmering water until the mixture starts to thicken. Divide the mixture between 6 glasses and chill.

In the same way – in a bowl over a pan of hot water, base not touching the water – melt the chocolate carefully. Add the cream, and stir well until smooth.

Put this on the top of the zabaglione. You can eat this straightaway or chill it again before serving.

6 organic egg yolks
120g caster sugar
170ml Moscato Passito di
    Pantelleria, Marsala or
    Madeira

Chocolate sauce
200g bitter chocolate, broken
    into pieces
100ml double cream

Tiramisu is now so internationally well known that it can be found absolutely everywhere. But this classic MOF MOF (Minimum of Fuss, Maximum of Flavour) recipe, which I created 30 years ago, is both simple and delicious. Try it, and you will discover that you instantly become a dessert maker!

MAKES 4 INDIVIDUAL TIRAMISUS

tiramisu

In a small bowl, beat the egg yolks, 80g of the caster sugar and the vanilla essence together. In a second larger bowl, mix the mascarpone with the cream to make it thinner. Mix the mascarpone with the egg. Should the mixture be too dense, add a few drops of milk.

Mix the coffee, chosen liqueur and remaining caster sugar together in a third bowl. Dip the biscuits briefly into the coffee (don't let them absorb too much liquid) and use to line 4 individual ramekins, cutting them in half if necessary to fit. Put in a layer of the mascarpone mixture, then top with some more biscuits, finishing with mascarpone and filling the ramekins to the top. Dust the tops with a little cocoa powder and chill until ready to serve.

2 egg yolks
100g caster sugar
a few drops of good
   vanilla essence
400g mascarpone cheese
80ml single cream
a little milk, if needed
400ml strong espresso coffee
4 tbsp Kahlua or Tia Maria
18 Savoyard biscuits (or ladies'
   fingers, they need to be
   absorbent)
some bitter cocoa powder, to dust

Italians love ricotta – a by-product of the cheese-making process – and use it to produce both savoury and sweet dishes. The most important thing to remember about ricotta is that it must always be very fresh: if there is even the tiniest hint of sourness, the ricotta is off. **SERVES 6–8**

ricotta
TART

Preheat the oven to 180°C/Gas 4. Grease the inside of a 25cm flan tin with a little of the butter, melting the remainder in a small pan over a low heat. Line the tin with the filo pastry, brushing each sheet with some of the melted butter.

Put the ricotta in a bowl, and loosen the texture with a fork. Mix in 100g of the sugar and the egg yolks, followed by the cubes of rind, the grated rind and the chocolate. Mix well together.

In another bowl, beat the egg whites until stiff, then add the remaining sugar. Fold this carefully into the ricotta mixture using a large metal spoon, taking care not to lose the airiness of the whipped whites.

Spread this filling on to the filo pastry on the base of the tin. Brush melted butter over the remaining sheet or sheets of filo. With scissors, cut ribbons of buttered filo pastry and spread these decoratively on the tart. Bake in the preheated oven for 30 minutes and, then take out and leave to cool before serving.

50g butter
3–4 sheets of filo pastry (frozen)

Filling
500g fresh ricotta cheese
120g caster sugar
5 eggs, separated
150g mix of orange and lemon rind, cut into small cubes
finely grated rind of 1 lemon
50g bitter chocolate, broken into small pieces

The most intensive taste of hazelnuts comes from the *tonda gentile delle Langhe*, a hazelnut grown in the Langhe region of Piedmont. The hazelnut itself is full of flavour, but becomes even more special after a gentle toasting.

SERVES 8

hazelnut
CAKE

Preheat the oven to 200°C/Gas 6. Use a little of the butter to grease a 25cm flan tin. Toast the hazelnuts on a baking tray in the preheated oven until a golden colour, a few minutes only. Cool and chop finely.

Soften the rest of the butter and beat together with 70g of the sugar in a large bowl. Add the egg yolks and beat until smooth, then add the flour and mix well. In another bowl, stir the ricotta with a fork until smooth. Add the cooled chopped hazelnuts and grated lemon rind.

Beat the egg whites separately in yet another bowl until stiff, then add the remaining sugar, beating until completely blended. Gently fold the yolk mixture into the white mixture with a large metal spoon until even, being careful to lose as little air from the whites as possible. Spoon or pour the cake mixture into the prepared tin and bake in the preheated oven for 30 minutes. Take out and leave the cake to cool in the tin.

When cool, remove the cake from the tin, and place on a cake plate. Spread the jam on top and sprinkle over the grated chocolate to finish.

100g unsalted butter
150g Piedmontese hazelnuts, shelled
125g caster sugar
4 large eggs, separated
30g plain flour
300g fresh ricotta cheese
1 tbsp finely grated lemon rind
200g apricot jam, slightly diluted with water
30g dark bitter chocolate, grated

I love polenta in every guise. In Piedmont where I spent my youth, there are many polenta biscuits, but none with the crispness I achieved by using *polenta svelta*, the quick polenta flour. These biscuits are wonderful as accompaniments to fresh fruit salads, or dipped into zabaglione. **MAKES ABOUT 50 BISCUITS**

polenta
BISCUITS

Preheat the oven to 200°C/Gas 6.

Mix all the ingredients together in a large bowl. Take a piping bag and fill it with the mixture. Pipe the mixture onto a greased baking tray in either little dots or S shapes. Leave a generous amount of space between the shapes as the biscuits will spread while cooking.

Bake in the preheated oven for 15 minutes, until golden.

Cool on a wire rack, and store in an airtight container.

200g unsalted butter, softened
200g granulated sugar
300g quick polenta
100g plain flour
½ tsp baking powder
4 eggs, beaten
finely grated zest of 1 lemon

At Christmas I brought a box of *pâté de fruit* from France – the little cubes dusted with sugar tasted of real fruit, inspired me to create this recipe. These pastels can be made with either home-made or commercial jam and eaten either as *petits fours*, or with cheese for lunch. **MAKES 120 PASTELS**

fruit
PASTELS

Put the jam and lemon juice in a pan and stir over a medium heat until the jam has softened and the mixture resembles a sticky paste.

Lightly grease a small ceramic tray with the oil, pour in the mixture and leave to cool. Cut the mixture into small cubes and roll each into walnut-sized balls. Dust with sugar before placing into paper *petits fours* cases.

1kg jam of any kind
juice of 1½ lemons
a little vegetable oil
caster sugar, to dust

INDEX

SPECIAL THANKS GO TO Alastair Hendy for the breathtaking photography; Anna Louise Naylor-Leyland and Martha Wailes for the endless typing; Susan Fleming for editing; Rebecca Hetherston for recipe testing. And to my agent Pat White, my publisher Quadrille and those who made the book possible: Alison Cathie, Jane O'Shea, Claire Peters, Simon Davis and Marina Asenjo.